# COLORADO TRIVIA

COMPILED BY B. J. MURPHEY-LENAHAN

Rutledge Hill Press
*Nashville, Tennessee*

Published by Rutledge Hill Press, Inc., 513 Third Avenue South, Nashville, Tennessee 37210

*Typography by Bailey Typography, Nashville, Tennessee*

**Library of Congress Cataloging-in-Publication Data**

Murphey-Lenahan, B. J., 1948-
    Colorado trivia / compiled by B. J. Murphey-Lenahan.
        p.    cm.
    ISBN 1-55853-135-1
    1. Colorado—Miscellanea.    2. Questions and answers.    I. Title.
F776.5.M87    1991
978.8—dc20                                                      91-33797
                                                                    CIP

Printed in the United States of America
2 3 4 5 6 7 8—98 97 96 95 94 93 92

# COLORADO TRIVIA

# PREFACE

Although Colorado is still known for its cowboys and Indians, it is also known as a popular tourist state with a wonderfully moderate climate. People from all over the world come to Colorado each year to ski, hunt, perform in plays, produce movies, or just enjoy the beautiful scenic sights.

Colorado is fast becoming a haven for people of the arts: actors, artists, writers, and recording artists. Its clear mountain air and relaxing pace of life can transport you back to a more peaceful existence without losing the flair for the latest in fashion or the arts. It's said that somewhere in Colorado is a place that anyone can gladly call home.

Q. Who coined the phrase "Only you can unlock the magic of your mind?"

A. Elizabeth P. Murphey (my mother).

Thanks also to my hubby, Tim, who still loves me and supported my work, my daughter Erin West, who worked as hard as I did in keeping this project going, and to my sons Bob and Tom Lenahan, and my other daughter Michelle. Thanks to Liz Patton for keeping me smiling, not an easy job at times, and a special thanks to Anne McCaffrey for being the gracious lady that she is and an inspiration to many. I love you all!

B. J.

# TABLE OF CONTENTS

# GEOGRAPHY

---

## C H A P T E R   O N E

---

Q. What do the names *Silent Friend, Snowstorm, Country Boy,* and *Kreutzer Sonata* have in common?

A. They are mining claims.

◆

Q. In what county are the Lowry Pueblo Ruins?

A. Montezuma.

◆

Q. By what other name is the Palmer Divide known?

A. Monument Hill.

◆

Q. How many people annually ascend Pikes Peak?

A. 400,000.

◆

Q. How much area does the Horsetooth Mountain Park cover?

A. 2,000 acres.

**Q.** What town was originally called Plaza of the Lions?

**A.** Walsenburg.

———◆———

**Q.** Along what area did the highest toll road in the nation once run?

**A.** The Continental Divide.

———◆———

**Q.** Where was the first Roman Catholic church in Colorado built?

**A.** Conejos (1857).

———◆———

**Q.** What is the nickname for the highway from Durango to Grand Junction?

**A.** The Million Dollar Road.

———◆———

**Q.** What is the name of the tunnel that is the site of the highest railroad in the country?

**A.** Needle's Eye.

———◆———

**Q.** Tepee Buttes are located north of what town?

**A.** Pueblo.

———◆———

**Q.** "Thunder Mountain," as the Indians called it, is in what national forest?

**A.** Grand Mesa National Forest.

**Q.** Where does one find Needle Rock?

**A.** Crawford.

———◆———

**Q.** The San Juan, Sangre de Cristo, and Sawatch mountains encircle what valley?

**A.** The San Luis.

———◆———

**Q.** What is the longest river in Colorado?

**A.** The Colorado.

———◆———

**Q.** The U.S. Air Force Academy encompasses how many acres?

**A.** 17,900.

———◆———

**Q.** What pass is the highest continuous automobile road in the United States?

**A.** Trail Ridge Road (U.S. 34).

———◆———

**Q.** In what county is the Black Mesa found?

**A.** Gunnison.

———◆———

**Q.** Colorado is known as the mother of what geographical feature?

**A.** Rivers.

Q. What Colorado river is 160 miles long?

A. The Gunnison.

———◆———

Q. What is the largest flat-topped mountain in the world?

A. The Grand Mesa.

———◆———

Q. Kokapelli's Trail runs 128 miles from Grand Junction to what other town?

A. Moab, Utah.

———◆———

Q. What kind of fascinating historical sites are at Hovenweep, Escalante, and Ute mountains?

A. Archaeological digs.

———◆———

Q. What Indian reservation covers a half-million acres?

A. The Ute Mountain Reservation.

———◆———

Q. The highest road in Colorado is on what peak?

A. Mount Evans.

———◆———

Q. Weather announcers frequently precede the name of what town with the word *freezin'*?

A. Frazier, as during the winter months it often is the coldest town in the nation.

**Q.** Where is the world's highest suspension bridge?

**A.** Over the Royal Gorge, near Canon City.

---

**Q.** What is the longest continuous street in America?

**A.** Colfax Avenue (Denver).

---

**Q.** What is the name of what was once the nation's smallest military installation before it moved to larger facilities?

**A.** ENT Air Force Base in Colorado Springs; it was one square block.

---

**Q.** What is the longest tunnel in the United States, at 8,959 feet?

**A.** E. Johnson Memorial on Interstate 70.

---

**Q.** What reporter of the New York *Tribune* helped in the discovery of Mesa Verde?

**A.** Ernest Ingersoll.

---

**Q.** By what nickname is Rangely known?

**A.** "Oil Basin."

---

**Q.** What forest near Colorado Springs has the same name as one in Germany?

**A.** The Black Forest.

Q. How long is the Colorado Trail?

A. 482 miles.

———◆———

Q. What is the official name for two land projections known as Rattlesnake Bluffs?

A. Pawnee Buttes.

———◆———

Q. Compared to other states, where does Colorado rank in size geographically?

A. Eighth.

———◆———

Q. How many counties does Colorado have?

A. Sixty-three.

———◆———

Q. To which mountain range do the Harvard, Yale, and Princeton mountains belong?

A. The Collegiate.

———◆———

Q. What was the standard size of a homestead?

A. 160 acres.

———◆———

Q. What river runs through Colorado, Utah, and Arizona?

A. The Colorado.

**Q.** The Garden of the Gods near Colorado Springs covers how many acres?

**A.** 770.

---

**Q.** Where is Navajo Lake?

**A.** Near Pagosa Springs.

---

**Q.** Burning Mountain is west of what town?

**A.** New Castle, where a fire has been burning in the Vulcan Mine since 1896.

---

**Q.** The north fork of the Big Thompson River flows into the Colorado River at what town?

**A.** Drake.

---

**Q.** The Dragon Spine was an Indian term referring to what area of Colorado?

**A.** The Rocky Mountains.

---

**Q.** The Game Creek Bowl is part of what area?

**A.** Vail ski resort.

---

**Q.** Where does Clear Creek meet South Clear Creek?

**A.** Georgetown.

**Q.** The town called Florissant was named after another Florissant of what state?

**A.** Missouri.

———◆———

**Q.** Leadville is in what county?

**A.** Lake.

———◆———

**Q.** Who founded Estes Park?

**A.** Joel Estes.

———◆———

**Q.** Mariano Medina settled what famous homestead, also known as Namaqua?

**A.** The Big Thompson Homestead.

———◆———

**Q.** What town is also known as Grand Valley?

**A.** Parachute.

———◆———

**Q.** What river fills the Eleven-mile Reservoir?

**A.** The South Platte.

———◆———

**Q.** What town, besides Golden, has a well-known brewery?

**A.** Fort Collins (Anheuser Busch, Inc.-Budweiser).

**Q.** In what county is Pool Table Mountain?

**A.** Rio Grande.

———◆———

**Q.** Which U.S. president signed the bill declaring Dinosaur Park a national monument?

**A.** Woodrow Wilson.

———◆———

**Q.** Douglas Pass is the headwaters of what major creek?

**A.** East Salt.

———◆———

**Q.** The headwaters of Beaver Creek are at what town?

**A.** Brush.

———◆———

**Q.** What is the name of the pass between Denver and Steamboat Springs?

**A.** Rabbit Ears.

———◆———

**Q.** What railroad runs between Antonito, Colorado, and Chama, New Mexico?

**A.** Cumbres-Toltec.

———◆———

**Q.** In what county are the headwaters of the Rio Grande River?

**A.** Mineral.

**Q.** What county is nicknamed "Criminal Inn"?

**A.** Fremont (because it has more prisons than any other county).

———◆———

**Q.** Bethune was named after a city in what nation?

**A.** France.

———◆———

**Q.** What is the primary industry at Naturita?

**A.** Mining.

———◆———

**Q.** What oil company built Battlement Mesa?

**A.** Exxon.

———◆———

**Q.** What is the maximum speed limit on Colorado county roads?

**A.** 45 MPH.

———◆———

**Q.** Where is Bent's Fort?

**A.** La Junta.

———◆———

**Q.** What is the elevation of the thirteenth step of the west entrance of the state capitol at Denver?

**A.** 5,280 feet (accounting for Denver's nickname, Mile High City).

**Q.** What natural occurrence 25 million years ago helped form the ore deposits in Mineral County?

**A.** Volcanic eruptions.

---◆---

**Q.** What canyon in western Colorado is narrower but deeper than the Grand Canyon?

**A.** Black.

---◆---

**Q.** What was the original name of Aurora?

**A.** Fletcher.

---◆---

**Q.** To what county do the Great Sand Dunes belong?

**A.** Alamosa.

---◆---

**Q.** How many square miles is the state of Colorado?

**A.** 104,247.

---◆---

**Q.** What proportion of Colorado land is owned by the federal government?

**A.** More than one-third.

---◆---

**Q.** What was the other name for the Platte Route used by the early prospectors?

**A.** The Oregon Trail.

# GEOGRAPHY

**Q.** What is the highest mountain pass in Colorado?

**A.** Independence Pass (12,095 feet).

———◆———

**Q.** What town was named after a type of grass?

**A.** Broomfield (broom-corn).

———◆———

**Q.** What town has the lowest altitude in Colorado at 3,397 feet?

**A.** Holly.

———◆———

**Q.** Poverty Gulch later became known as what town?

**A.** Cripple Creek.

———◆———

**Q.** What town, with an altitude of 10,188 feet, is said to be the highest incorporated city in the United States?

**A.** Leadville.

———◆———

**Q.** What does the Spanish word *colorado* mean?

**A.** "Colored red."

———◆———

**Q.** At 14,433 feet, what is the highest mountain in Colorado?

**A.** Mount Elbert.

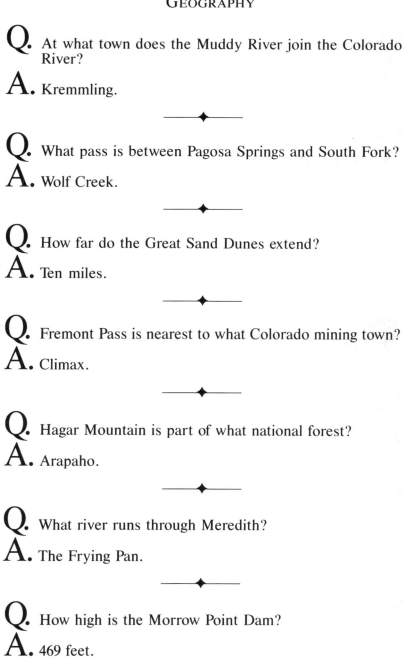

**Q.** At what town does the Muddy River join the Colorado River?

**A.** Kremmling.

---

**Q.** What pass is between Pagosa Springs and South Fork?

**A.** Wolf Creek.

---

**Q.** How far do the Great Sand Dunes extend?

**A.** Ten miles.

---

**Q.** Fremont Pass is nearest to what Colorado mining town?

**A.** Climax.

---

**Q.** Hagar Mountain is part of what national forest?

**A.** Arapaho.

---

**Q.** What river runs through Meredith?

**A.** The Frying Pan.

---

**Q.** How high is the Morrow Point Dam?

**A.** 469 feet.

**Q.** How many miles long is the Black Canyon?

**A.** Fifty-three.

---

**Q.** What pass is the gateway to Middle Park?

**A.** Berthoud.

---

**Q.** What town lies below Cannibal Plateau?

**A.** Lake City.

---

**Q.** What is Colorado's northernmost town?

**A.** Slater.

---

**Q.** What highway runs between Canon City and Delta?

**A.** U.S. 50.

---

**Q.** How high above the San Luis Valley do the Great Sand Dunes rise?

**A.** 700 feet.

---

**Q.** What project was started in 1978 to store and provide water for Montezuma and Dolores counties?

**A.** The Dolores River Project.

Q. Near what pass is the Elk Track War Lodge?

A. Cochetopa.

---◆---

Q. What river runs through the Black Canyon?

A. The Gunnison.

---◆---

Q. When was the name of the town Fletcher changed to Aurora?

A. 1901.

---◆---

Q. What two streets that run side by side in Denver also run side by side in Indianapolis, Indiana?

A. Fenton and Gibson.

---◆---

Q. What canyon is four miles west of Cortez?

A. Crow.

---◆---

Q. On what mountain pass is the Muleshoe?

A. Old La Veta.

---◆---

Q. Wagon Wheel Gap is in what county?

A. Mineral.

**Q.** What reservoir is near Willow Reservoir?

**A.** Heart.

———◆———

**Q.** How far is Gunnison from Canon City?

**A.** 221 miles.

———◆———

**Q.** Lincoln Park is considered a suburb of what town?

**A.** Canon City.

———◆———

**Q.** What town near Westcliffe was originally settled by a large number of German immigrants?

**A.** Rosita.

———◆———

**Q.** Who founded the model industrial village Crystal River Valley, now the town of Redstone?

**A.** John Cleveland Osgood.

———◆———

**Q.** Each year hundreds of thousands of valentines are sent to what Colorado city for remailing?

**A.** Loveland.

———◆———

**Q.** What town is at the beginning of Trail Ridge Road?

**A.** Estes Park.

Q. What is the name of the 14,294-foot peak just north of the Great Sand Dunes?

A. Crestone.

———◆———

Q. What is the name of the scenic road between Colorado Springs and Cripple Creek?

A. Gold Camp.

———◆———

Q. Where does the south end of Shelf Road start?

A. Canon City.

———◆———

Q. What trail was once a migratory route for buffalo?

A. Cochetopa Pass.

———◆———

Q. What town is considered the Hummingbird Capital of the world?

A. Empire.

———◆———

Q. Where is the office of the state archaeologist?

A. Denver.

———◆———

Q. Antero Peak is a part of what mountain range?

A. The San Juan.

Q. Trout Creek Pass is the gateway to what valley?

A. The upper Arkansas.

———◆———

Q. During the 1860s, what town was known as the richest square mile on earth?

A. Central City.

———◆———

Q. What was the first town in Colorado to have electric lights?

A. Aspen.

———◆———

Q. What was the original name of Montrose?

A. Pamona.

———◆———

Q. What 2,164-foot-long tunnel, at an altitude of 11,528 feet, serves the highest standard-gauge railroad in the nation?

A. The Haggerman (near Leadville).

———◆———

Q. What mine was started on the advice of a spiritualist?

A. The Highland Mary.

———◆———

Q. What county lies between Moffat, Jackson, and Grand counties?

A. Routt.

**Q.** The town of Springfield is on the northern edge of what national grassland?

**A.** Comanche (southern unit).

---

**Q.** What Colorado river feeds into the John Martin Reservoir?

**A.** The Arkansas.

---

**Q.** What famous trail runs near Campo?

**A.** The Chisholm.

---

**Q.** The Moffat Tunnel made possible the 175-mile throughway from Denver to what other city?

**A.** Salt Lake City.

---

**Q.** Where is Bartlett Mountain?

**A.** Leadville.

---

**Q.** What town was named after a character created by Sir Walter Scott?

**A.** Montrose (after the duchess of Montrose).

---

**Q.** What is Aurora's nickname?

**A.** The "Gateway to the Rockies."

Q. What town received its name because it was situated at the highest elevation of the Denver & Rio Grande Railroad?

A. Climax.

———◆———

Q. The Colorado State Hospital is in what town?

A. Pueblo.

———◆———

Q. Where is the Colorado Boys Ranch?

A. La Junta.

———◆———

Q. What Indian chief had a county named after him?

A. Chief Ouray.

———◆———

Q. What town is nearest to the Green Mountain Reservoir?

A. Campo.

———◆———

Q. Horse Mountain is part of what national forest?

A. Grand Mesa.

———◆———

Q. Sapinero borders what reservoir?

A. Blue Mesa.

Q. At Cordell, gold miners drilled into what unusual geological formation?

A. An extinct volcano.

———◆———

Q. Where is the Kit Carson County Fairgrounds?

A. Burlington.

———◆———

Q. What kind of disaster twice destroyed the town of Creed?

A. Fire.

———◆———

Q. What do Flattop, Hallett, Otis, Taylor, Thatchtop, and Chief's Head have in common?

A. All are mountain peaks, part of the Continental Divide.

———◆———

Q. What was the original name of Lakewood?

A. Jefferson City.

———◆———

Q. What was the occupation of Robert Chambers, for whom Chambers Lake was named?

A. Trapper.

———◆———

Q. Who constructed the nature trail in the Fort Collins Mountain Park?

A. The Rocky Mountain Climbers Club.

Q. Through what gap flow the waters of the Middle Fork of the Purgatory River?

A. Stonewall.

———◆———

Q. What is the only national forest in Colorado where the aspen tree is not indigenous?

A. The San Juan.

———◆———

Q. Cameron Pass lies between Mount Richthofen and what peak?

A. Clark.

———◆———

Q. Why was the state given the name *Colorado*?

A. It is derived from the Spanish for "colored red."

———◆———

Q. What is the official name of the pass known as the "Highway of Frozen Death"?

A. Mosquito Pass.

———◆———

Q. Beside what river is the town of Bedrock?

A. The Dolores.

———◆———

Q. What was the native country of George Gore, for whom Gore Mountain was named?

A. Ireland.

**Q.** What is the chief occupation of the people who live in the Kremmling area?

**A.** Ranching.

———◆———

**Q.** Where are the Seven Falls located?

**A.** Colorado Springs.

———◆———

**Q.** What is unique about the southwesternmost corner of Colorado?

**A.** It is the only point in the United States common to four states.

———◆———

**Q.** What beer company operates out of Golden?

**A.** Coors.

———◆———

**Q.** The British earl of Dunraven once held ownership of 15,000 acres in what area?

**A.** Estes Park.

———◆———

**Q.** Who named Echo Park?

**A.** John Wesley Powell.

———◆———

**Q.** Where are the Sleeping Ute Mountains?

**A.** Cortez.

Q. Where is the Molly Kathleen Mine?

A. Cripple Creek.

———————◆———————

Q. What river runs through Florence?

A. The Arkansas.

———————◆———————

Q. How many acres of crystal clear lakes are there at Rainbow Falls Park?

A. Twenty-five.

———————◆———————

Q. Where is the Cave of the Winds?

A. Manitou Springs.

———————◆———————

Q. What town is the "Gateway to Grand Mesa"?

A. Cedaredge.

———————◆———————

Q. Where is America's only mountain zoo?

A. Cheyenne Mountain.

———————◆———————

Q. Where are the world's hottest mineral springs?

A. Pagosa Springs.

**Q.** A stuffed rooster by the name of T. J. Flournoy, originally from a house of ill repute in La Grange, Texas, now resides in what city?

**A.** Cripple Creek, at the Red Rooster Bar of the Imperial Hotel.

---

**Q.** Where do Interstate 70 and State Highway 50 meet?

**A.** Grand Junction.

---

**Q.** Where is Ames College?

**A.** Greeley.

---

**Q.** What Swiss-made train makes a scenic round trip of the mountainous area around Manitou Springs?

**A.** The Pikes Peak Cog Railway.

---

**Q.** In what county are Vallecito Lake and Lemon Reservoir?

**A.** Montezuma.

---

**Q.** The Overland Reservoir is in what national forest?

**A.** Grand Mesa.

---

**Q.** Gold Creek runs through what Colorado town?

**A.** Ohio.

**Q.** What junior college has campuses in Glenwood Springs, Leadville, and Steamboat Springs?

**A.** Colorado Mountain College.

---

**Q.** Where is Engine No. 60, a Rhode Island 2-8-0 steam engine?

**A.** Idaho Springs.

---

**Q.** What is the correct name of the "Lazy Ranch" in Aspen?

**A.** The T-Lazy-Seven Ranch.

---

**Q.** What is Ashcroft (near Aspen) currently known as?

**A.** A ghost town.

---

**Q.** What river flows into the Lemon Dam?

**A.** The Florida.

---

**Q.** What government agency administers 14.4 million acres of land in Colorado, including twelve national forests and two national grasslands?

**A.** The Forest Service.

---

**Q.** What body of water runs past the town of Wild Horse?

**A.** The Big Sandy Creek.

Q. Colorado contains what percentage of the land area of the United States with an altitude over 10,000 feet?

A. 75 percent.

----◆----

Q. How many state wildlife areas are there in Colorado?

A. 222.

----◆----

Q. In what county is Williams Creek Reservoir?

A. Hindsdale.

----◆----

Q. How many designated wilderness areas are there in Colorado?

A. Twenty-five.

----◆----

Q. What is the special designation of more than 150 miles of streams and 566 acres of lakes?

A. Designated Wild Trout Waters.

----◆----

Q. How many state wildlife refuges are there in Colorado?

A. Four (Alamosa, Monte Vista, Arapaho, and Brown's Park).

----◆----

Q. The 55,647 acres of land administered by the National Park Service are also part of what other national system?

A. National Wilderness Preservation System.

**Q.** Where is the main office for the Colorado Forest Service?

**A.** Lakewood.

———◆———

**Q.** How many state parks are there in Colorado?

**A.** Thirty-five.

———◆———

**Q.** In what town is Doc Holliday's grave?

**A.** Glenwood Springs.

———◆———

**Q.** What do Leadville and Hotchkiss have in common concerning fish?

**A.** Both have national fish hatcheries.

———◆———

**Q.** Where can one see 20,445 acres of sandstone monoliths and red rock canyons?

**A.** Rim Rock Drive.

———◆———

**Q.** On what cliffs are preserved traces from the Eocene Age?

**A.** Vermillion Cliffs (in the multistrata of the Wasatch Formation).

———◆———

**Q.** What is Colorado's second-largest lake?

**A.** Trapper's Lake.

Q. Rangely is best known for what 1902 discovery that is unique for its geological make up?

A. High-gravity crude oil.

———◆———

Q. What state recreation area is approximately ten miles east of Palisade?

A. Island Acres.

———◆———

Q. What town is called the Outdoor Capital of Colorado?

A. Dolores.

———◆———

Q. How many lakes connect in the Curecanti National Recreation Area?

A. Three (the Blue Mesa, Morrow Point, and Crystal).

———◆———

Q. How many state fish hatcheries are there in Colorado?

A. Thirteen.

———◆———

Q. What was the first county designated in Colorado?

A. Denver.

———◆———

Q. What is considered to be the archaeological center of the United States?

A. Cortez.

**Q.** Where is the Tamarron Resort?

**A.** Durango.

---

**Q.** What town is known as the "City of Murals"?

**A.** Delta.

---

**Q.** When did the Cave of the Winds open?

**A.** February 15, 1881.

---

**Q.** What town is the "Gem of the Rockies"?

**A.** Ouray.

---

**Q.** Where can you play a good game of checkers, see a melodrama, eat a cowboy-cooked sixteen-ounce steak, and meet a dog named Nevada?

**A.** The General Store (south of Canon City).

---

**Q.** In what county is Castlewood Canyon State Park?

**A.** Douglas.

---

**Q.** Where is the Arabian Horse Center?

**A.** Denver.

Q. What Colorado town is designated the "small town with a big heart"?

A. Nederland.

---

Q. Where is the "Banana Belt" of Colorado?

A. The Arkansas Valley.

---

Q. Where does the West meet the Southwest?

A. Alamosa.

---

Q. What town is at the geographic center of Colorado?

A. Fairplay.

---

Q. How many Indian reservations are there in Colorado?

A. Two.

---

Q. What is the name of the castle near Rye?

A. Bishop Castle.

---

Q. What town is known as the City of Mills?

A. Black Hawk.

Q. What is the nearest town to the Great Sand Dunes?

A. Red Wing.

——◆——

Q. In what county is the Comanche National Grasslands?

A. Crowley.

——◆——

Q. What are the Nee So Pah, Nee Grande, Nee Noshe, and Nee Shah?

A. Reservoirs.

——◆——

Q. Where is Fort Lewis College?

A. Durango.

——◆——

Q. What river runs by Greeley?

A. The Platte.

——◆——

Q. Where is the Lion House of the Anasazi?

A. Near Mesa Verde.

——◆——

Q. How far underground in Cheyenne Mountain is the combat operations center headquarters of the North American Air Defense Command (NORAD)?

A. 1,200 feet.

# ENTERTAINMENT

## C H A P T E R   T W O

Q. Kent Groshong and Larry Zimmer are radio personalities at what Denver station?

A. KOA.

------◆------

Q. In 1895 the town of Gillette hosted what unusual sport?

A. A bull fight (the first and last for Colorado).

------◆------

Q. What James Bond movie featured a house, built near
Idaho Springs, that looks like a flying saucer?

A. *For Your Eyes Only.*

------◆------

Q. What former Disney actor and former "Laugh-In"
actress live near Aspen?

A. Kurt Russell and Goldie Hawn.

------◆------

Q. What lawyer movies are filmed for television in Denver
and neighboring cities?

A. Perry Mason.

Q. What well-known hotel was the setting for the movie *The Shining*?

A. The Stanley Hotel in Estes Park.

———◆———

Q. What musical starring Lee Marvin and Clint Eastwood was filmed in part near Black Hawk?

A. *Paint Your Wagon.*

———◆———

Q. Where are medieval times relived each summer?

A. At the Larkspur Renaissance.

———◆———

Q. How many movies have been filmed at Buckskin Joe, a reconstructed mining town?

A. Thirteen.

———◆———

Q. What Colorado shrine was built as a monument to Will Rogers?

A. The Shrine of the Sun, a few miles above the Cheyenne Mountain Zoo.

———◆———

Q. What television series, supposedly set in Chicago, was originally filmed in Denver?

A. "Father Dowling Mysteries."

———◆———

Q. What was Colorado's first television station?

A. KFEL, Denver.

Q. Who was the first country music artist to perform live on Colorado radio?

A. Captain Ozzie Waters and the Ford Rangers (on KOA).

———◆———

Q. What radio station was the first in Colorado to go full-time country?

A. KLAK, in Lakewood.

———◆———

Q. What Denver radio personality was East Tin Cup's most famous mayor?

A. Pete Smyth.

———◆———

Q. Where was Magic Mountain Amusement Park situated?

A. Near Golden.

———◆———

Q. What opera describes life during the great Colorado mining boom?

A. *The Ballad of Baby Doe.*

———◆———

Q. Where is the Colorado Shakespeare Festival held each summer?

A. Mary Rippon Outdoor Theatre, University of Colorado, Boulder.

———◆———

Q. Where is the forty-six-room Miramont Castle?

A. Maniton Springs.

Q. What is the oldest ride at Elitch Gardens Amusement Park?

A. The carousel.

———◆———

Q. Bill Fries, the mayor of Ouray, is known by what other name?

A. C. W. McCall (commercial actor and singer).

———◆———

Q. What well-loved Denverite throws a free Thanksgiving dinner for Denver's needy?

A. Daddy Bruce.

———◆———

Q. Where did television's Mork from Ork live on earth?

A. Boulder.

———◆———

Q. What former president has a home in Aspen?

A. Gerald Ford.

———◆———

Q. What pop singing star performed on his birthday in 1985 at Denver's Mile High Stadium?

A. Bruce Springsteen.

———◆———

Q. What western-movie star got his start in Canon City in a 1910 silent movie?

A. Tom Mix.

**Q.** What formally occupied the site of Denver's prestigious Cherry Hills Shopping Center?

**A.** A dump.

———◆———

**Q.** What was the name of Denver's first entertainment hall, built in the mid-1800s by Libeus Barney?

**A.** The Apollo.

———◆———

**Q.** Where is Colorado's oldest vineyard?

**A.** Palisade (the Colorado Cellars).

———◆———

**Q.** What was made in 1905 by the Philadlephia Toboggan Company and is now used in Burlington?

**A.** A carousel.

———◆———

**Q.** The *Encyclopedia Britannica* commissioned what Colorado-born actor to write the article on theatrical makeup in its fourteenth edition?

**A.** Lon Chaney.

———◆———

**Q.** Eldorado Springs is known for what particular form of enjoyment?

**A.** Spa of Thermal Springs.

———◆———

**Q.** Who built the Broadmoor Hotel?

**A.** Spencer Penrose.

Q. What movie was filmed in Estes Park in 1983?

A. *Dear Desperado.*

◆

Q. Where is Watermelon Day an annual celebration?

A. Rocky Ford.

◆

Q. What was John Elitch, founder of Elitch Gardens, also known for?

A. His Tortoni Restaurant.

◆

Q. The television show "That's Incredible" featured a segment about what Colorado bridge?

A. The Royal Gorge, the world's highest suspension bridge.

◆

Q. What was the name of the first television network affiliation in Denver?

A. Dumont Television Network.

◆

Q. What well-known radio personality helped investigate the story of Bridey Murphy?

A. Bill Barker.

◆

Q. What famous Aurora country-western night club burned down in 1985?

A. The Four Seasons.

Q. What famous saxophone player headed the entertainment at the 1979 Pro-Rocky Flats Rally?

A. Boots Randolph.

---

Q. In what town is the Victorian Hotel Gilpin?

A. Black Hawk.

---

Q. Bat Masterson, Helen Keller, Simon and Garfunkel, and Theodore Roosevelt stayed at what hotel in Boulder?

A. The Boulderado, built in 1908.

---

Q. What year did Hal Holbrook perform his one-man show about Mark Twain at the Boulder Theater?

A. 1983.

---

Q. What Victorian hotel claims to have a resident ghost named George who likes to light candles and slam doors?

A. The Redstone Inn.

---

Q. Where can you find a diner shaped like a hot dog?

A. Conifer.

---

Q. What is the name of the oldest summer stock theater in the United States?

A. Elitch Theatre (opened in 1891).

Q. The Professional Rodeo Hall of Fame is in what city?

A. Colorado Springs.

◆

Q. What television soap opera was set in Denver?

A. "Dynasty."

◆

Q. What is the name of the breathtaking roller coaster ride at Elitch Gardens?

A. The Wildcat.

◆

Q. What Denver-born boy who hated to practice his viola later became America's King of Jazz?

A. Paul Whiteman.

◆

Q. What Union Pacific steam locomotive still makes an annual run from Cheyenne, Wyoming, to Denver?

A. Number 8444.

◆

Q. What Colorado band was in Clint Eastwood's movie, *Every Which Way But Loose*?

A. Lee Simmes and the Platte River Band.

◆

Q. What actor from the movie *Batman* has a home in Aspen?

A. Jack Nicholson.

Q. The annual Carousel Ball benefits what charity?

A. Children's Diabetes.

◆

Q. What actor, who portrayed a vampire in the movie *Love at First Bite,* has a home in Colorado?

A. George Hamilton.

◆

Q. Along what river was the movie *Centennial* filmed?

A. The Platte (near Platteville).

◆

Q. Where is the Matawin Village Tepee Camp for Children?

A. Beaver Creek Mountain.

◆

Q. In what resort is Clancy's Windy City Irish Pub of the Cascade Village?

A. Vail.

◆

Q. What town hosts the Aspenfest?

A. Georgetown.

◆

Q. Who directed the play *Harvey,* written by Denver playwright Mary Chase?

A. Antoinette Perry.

Q. The Stone Quarries and Petroglyphs Tour operates in what county?

A. Rio Grande.

———◆———

Q. What famous female television interviewer has a home in Aspen?

A. Barbara Walters.

———◆———

Q. What festival is held each fall in Denver's Larimer Square?

A. Oktoberfest.

———◆———

Q. Where is Zebulon Pike's sword on display?

A. Colorado State Historical Museum.

———◆———

Q. The Moon Run Outfitters do business at what resort?

A. Aspen (for pack trips, fishing, and hunting).

———◆———

Q. Where is the Crystal Palace dinner theater?

A. Aspen.

———◆———

Q. What is the name of the wild roller coaster ride at Lakeside Amusement Park?

A. The Cyclone.

Q. Where can one join an actual trail drive, called the North Branch of the Santa Fe Trail?

A. San Luis Valley.

———◆———

Q. Where is Colorado's "North Pole"?

A. On Pikes Peak.

———◆———

Q. The Colorado State Fair is held each year in what city?

A. Pueblo.

———◆———

Q. What resident of Aspen sang in the 1984 Olympics?

A. John Denver.

———◆———

Q. Where was radio and television personality Ralph Edwards born?

A. Merino.

———◆———

Q. In what part of Colorado was a portion of the movie *American Flyers* filmed?

A. The Rocky Mountains.

———◆———

Q. What popular singer was married in Redstone Castle?

A. Jimmy Buffett.

Q. What is the nickname of McNickols Sports Arena?

A. Big Mac.

———◆———

Q. What are Rocky Mountain oysters?

A. Fried bull testicles.

———◆———

Q. What was the name of the backup band for Kenny Brent?

A. The Texas Express.

———◆———

Q. What was the largest single amount won in the Colorado lotto in 1990?

A. Eleven million dollars.

———◆———

Q. In what Colorado town was actor Jan-Michael Vincent born on July 15, 1944?

A. Denver.

———◆———

Q. What Denver Broncos player made a recording about the Broncos?

A. John Keyworth.

———◆———

Q. One of the more colorful panelists of "The Gong Show," Jaye P. Morgan, was from what Colorado town?

A. Mancos.

**Q.** What occasional actor on the "Andy Griffith Show" was from Bethune?

**A.** Denver Pyle.

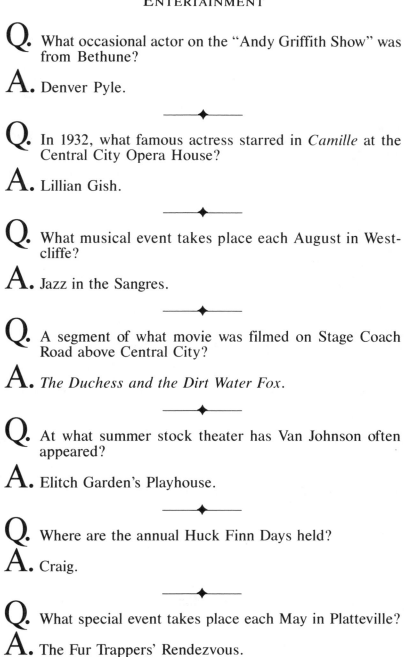

**Q.** In 1932, what famous actress starred in *Camille* at the Central City Opera House?

**A.** Lillian Gish.

**Q.** What musical event takes place each August in Westcliffe?

**A.** Jazz in the Sangres.

**Q.** A segment of what movie was filmed on Stage Coach Road above Central City?

**A.** *The Duchess and the Dirt Water Fox.*

**Q.** At what summer stock theater has Van Johnson often appeared?

**A.** Elitch Garden's Playhouse.

**Q.** Where are the annual Huck Finn Days held?

**A.** Craig.

**Q.** What special event takes place each May in Platteville?

**A.** The Fur Trappers' Rendezvous.

**Q.** Where is the Pick-n-Hoe Celebration held annually on July 4?

**A.** Dove Creek.

◆

**Q.** What town hosts a tick festival?

**A.** Heeney.

◆

**Q.** What famous "Hawaii Five-O" actor lives in the Crested Butte area?

**A.** James McArthur.

◆

**Q.** When did Elitch Gardens first open its gates?

**A.** 1891.

◆

**Q.** Where are Bloom Days, which feature an international pack burro race?

**A.** Leadville.

◆

**Q.** Where did the Platte River Band play for many years in Denver?

**A.** The Zanzibar.

◆

**Q.** What Burlington activity draws people from across the country to ride twenty miles from Main Street to Old Town?

**A.** The Longhorn Cattle Drive.

**Q.** Where can one attend a Cherry Blossom festival complete with Japanese food at a Buddhist temple?

**A.** Denver.

––––––◆––––––

**Q.** What three-day artisans' fair with live entertainment takes place in Glenwood Springs?

**A.** Strawberry Days Festival.

––––––◆––––––

**Q.** What ski area features a dual fiberglass track for wheeled sleds?

**A.** Breckenridge.

––––––◆––––––

**Q.** What is the name of the special event in Leadville that re-creates an old mining camp?

**A.** Oro City.

––––––◆––––––

**Q.** Why is Lou Bunch remembered with Lou Bunch Day in Central City?

**A.** She was the city's last madam.

––––––◆––––––

**Q.** Ignacio hosts what annual tribal festivity?

**A.** Southern Ute Tribal Bear Dance.

––––––◆––––––

**Q.** What show was featured at the 1991 Littleton Riverfront Festival?

**A.** *The Music Man.*

Q. What was the main attraction at the 1991 United States Air Force Academy graduation?

A. The Thunderbirds Air Show.

———◆———

Q. Where does the four-wheel-drive Wheeler Monument tour start?

A. Del Norte.

———◆———

Q. Where are the Rocky Mountain Street Rod Nationals held?

A. Pueblo.

———◆———

Q. At what airfield is the Aspen Air Show of vintage airplanes held?

A. Sardy Field.

———◆———

Q. What movie starring Burt Reynolds was filmed in Denver and concerned the Denver mint?

A. *Sam Whiskey.*

———◆———

Q. What group performed at the 53rd Annual Broadmoor Ice Review in Colorado Springs?

A. The Broadmoor Skating Club.

———◆———

Q. What is the Old West's largest theme park?

A. Buckskin Joe Park and Railway.

**Q.** What is the name of the Montrose wine tasting and culinary extravaganza?

**A.** The Altrusa Lawn Party.

———◆———

**Q.** What group was featured at the 1991 Crested Butte Chamber Music Festival?

**A.** Ted Piltzecker Jazz Quintet.

———◆———

**Q.** What Golden museum houses such 1880s antiques as telegraphers' instruments and a wooden water tower?

**A.** The Colorado Railroad Museum.

———◆———

**Q.** Who was Professor K-How?

**A.** Dave Baysinger (KHOW Radio).

———◆———

**Q.** Where in Cortez can one witness traditional Indian dances every week during the summer?

**A.** The city park.

———◆———

**Q.** Where is the Red Ryder Rodeo held?

**A.** Pagosa Springs.

———◆———

**Q.** As of 1991, how many years has the world-famous Denver International Film Festival been held?

**A.** Fourteen.

Q. What is the name of the thirteen-foot focal length lens offering a magnified panorama of the Garden of the Gods?

A. Camera Obscura.

———◆———

Q. Where is the Gold Bar Room Theatre that stages old-fashioned melodramas?

A. Imperial Hotel, Cripple Creek.

———◆———

Q. Where was *How the West Was Won* filmed?

A. Ouray.

———◆———

Q. In what town can one eat buffalo at the Buffalo Bar?

A. Idaho Springs.

———◆———

Q. Where is the Balloons, Blues & Barbecue held in July?

A. Vail.

———◆———

Q. What fund-raiser, held in Olathe for injured loggers, features competitions in pole climbing and saw cutting?

A. Loggers' Days.

———◆———

Q. What festival in Como is dedicated to the early explorers of the region?

A. Mountain Man Rendezvous.

**Q.** Where are the Donkey Derby Days held?

**A.** Cripple Creek.

———◆———

**Q.** Where does the annual Collegiate Peaks Rodeo take place?

**A.** Buena Vista.

———◆———

**Q.** Where can one observe blacksmithing, quilting, and other demonstrations of pioneer life during Ute Pass Days?

**A.** Cascade.

———◆———

**Q.** Where is the U.S. Space Symposium held each April?

**A.** Colorado Springs.

———◆———

**Q.** Who performed at Red Rocks Amphitheater on August 25, 1964?

**A.** The Beatles.

———◆———

**Q.** What two-day workshop featuring identification of edible and poisonous mountain mushrooms takes place in Creede?

**A.** Creede Mushroom Foray.

———◆———

**Q.** Where is a local fair called the Tumblewood Festival held?

**A.** Cheyenne Wells.

Q. What is the name of the group of Denver policemen who are musicians?

A. The Lawmen.

———◆———

Q. What children's television character in Denver also owns an antique store?

A. Blinky the Clown.

———◆———

Q. What Denver radio talk show host was gunned down outside his home in 1984?

A. Alan Berg.

———◆———

Q. What station in Denver has been showing reruns of original "Star Trek" episodes longer than any other station in Colorado?

A. KWGN (Channel 2).

———◆———

Q. Where does Cher have a part-time home?

A. Aspen.

———◆———

Q. Where did Claire Bloom do readings of Shakespeare as a one-women show in 1991?

A. The Boulder Theater.

———◆———

Q. Where is the annual Scottish Highland Festival held?

A. Estes Park.

Q. During the tourist season, in what town does the mayor's wife play a madam at the Old Town's Longhorn Saloon?

A. Burlington.

―――◆―――

Q. Who founded the Cowboy Turtle Association?

A. Hugh Bennett.

―――◆―――

Q. Where in Denver did the play *Harvey* appear in 1977?

A. The Country Dinner Playhouse.

―――◆―――

Q. Where do the Boondocks Players perform a series of one-act comedies?

A. Dumont.

―――◆―――

Q. Where does the Black American West Museum and Heritage 5 Km Run/Walk start?

A. Denver City Park.

―――◆―――

Q. Harry W. Cooke was the first to receive what degree from Denver University?

A. Law.

―――◆―――

Q. What native of Fairplay is the mountaineering instructor for the Colorado Outward Bound school?

A. Gary E. Nichols.

**Q.** Where in Colorado do Robert Wagner and Jill St. John have a home?

**A.** Aspen.

———◆———

**Q.** What hotel has the unique telephone number 1-800-ROCKIES?

**A.** The Stanley Hotel (Estes Park).

———◆———

**Q.** Where is the annual Stone Age Fair?

**A.** Loveland.

———◆———

**Q.** What is the name of the annual celebration in Estes Park featuring carolers, puppets, live window mannequins, and a nighttime parade of music and lights?

**A.** Catch the Glow.

———◆———

**Q.** Juneteenth in Denver is a celebration of what memorable event?

**A.** The end of slavery in Texas.

———◆———

**Q.** Where is the July Buffalo Barbecue?

**A.** Morrison.

———◆———

**Q.** The Annual Air Show of Colorado at the Front Range Airport is held in what town?

**A.** Watkins.

Q. What military re-enactment takes place at Fort Garland?

A. 1880s Military Encampment.

———◆———

Q. In what town can one attend the Under the Big Top Antique Show and Sale?

A. Morrison.

———◆———

Q. What western movie starring Glenn Campbell and John Wayne was filmed in Ridgeway?

A. *True Grit*.

———◆———

Q. In what entertainment medium is Don Roberts best known?

A. Radio.

———◆———

Q. Who are Hal Moore and Charlie Martin?

A. Radio personalities (KHOW-Denver).

———◆———

Q. What Denver television weatherman was once introduced in the on-air lead-in as "What's-his-name"?

A. Larry Green.

———◆———

Q. In 1979, who canceled a performance at Red Rocks Amphitheater because of rain but returned the next day to perform in the rain?

A. Waylon Jennings.

Q. What movie starring Ida Lupino used the Rio Grande dining car Pikes Peak, from the Forney Museum in Denver?

A. *Man Hunter*.

———◆———

Q. Where in Colorado does Buddy Hackett have a home?

A. Aspen.

———◆———

Q. Who sponsors the English Riding-Hunter/Jumper Show in Dumont?

A. The Clear Creek Rodeo Horseman's Association.

———◆———

Q. Where is the "Eenie Weenie Bikini Ski Contest?

A. Copper Mountain.

———◆———

Q. What actress who appeared in the *Wizard of Oz* filmed commercials in Denver?

A. Margaret Hamilton.

———◆———

Q. Who is Little Johnny Harding?

A. A Denver radio personality.

———◆———

Q. What is the only clear channel radio station in Colorado?

A. KOA.

Q. At what radio station were Jockey Joe, Perry Martin, and Sandy Travis?

A. KLZ–AM.

———◆———

Q. In what town can one witness a frog rodeo?

A. Empire.

———◆———

Q. What woman psychic made a name for herself on radio KIMN in Denver?

A. Lou Wright.

———◆———

Q. What movie starring Johnny Cash used the Rio Grande dining car Pikes Peak?

A. *Riding the Rails.*

———◆———

Q. Why did Buffalo Bill fire Calamity Jane from his Wild West Show?

A. For drunkenness.

———◆———

Q. What was the name of the Heritage Square Music Hall prior to 1989?

A. The Heritage Square Opera House.

———◆———

Q. When was the Sangre de Cristo Arts and Conference Center opened?

A. 1972.

**Q.** Where is the Turkey Shoot Weekend held?

**A.** Strasburg.

---◆---

**Q.** What is the correct name of Denver's planetarium?

**A.** The Charles C. Gates Planetarium.

---◆---

**Q.** Who were Rose Mary Barnwell and the late Buzz Lawrence?

**A.** Buzz & Barney of KHOW radio.

---◆---

**Q.** What was the original name of the Boulder Theater?

**A.** The Curran Opera House.

---◆---

**Q.** Where is the 1927 Mercedes-Benz car, adapted for a wheelchair, which was confiscated by the U.S. government from the German ambassador at the beginning of WWII?

**A.** The Forney Museum in Denver.

---◆---

**Q.** With whom did Bill Haley and the Comets perform in Denver in 1973?

**A.** Chuck Berry.

---◆---

**Q.** What owner-actor appears at the Heritage Square Music Hall?

**A.** T. J. Mullin.

Q. What country-western singer overdosed in Denver in the 1970s, yet survived?

A. Hank Williams, Jr.

---

Q. What is the name of Denver's big science fiction conference, held the last week of each October?

A. The Mile High Con.

---

Q. In 1990, what country music star lost his home in Evergreen because of unpaid taxes?

A. Willie Nelson.

---

Q. What role did Leonard Nimoy play at the Denver Auditorium in 1975?

A. Sherlock Holmes.

---

Q. Where in Denver was the first Star Trek Convention held?

A. The Sheridan Hotel (1976).

---

Q. How long is the average St. Patrick's Day parade in Denver?

A. Four hours.

---

Q. What comedian-singer bombed in Idaho Springs and had to have his mother wire him money to get back home?

A. Groucho Marx.

Q. At the 1991 Star Trek Convention in Denver, who was the star guest from the original series?

A. James Doohan, "Scotty."

———◆———

Q. How many times have the Beach Boys performed at the Colorado State Fair?

A. Two.

———◆———

Q. In what production did Katherine Hepburn perform in Denver 1976 despite a broken leg?

A. *The Importance of Being Ernest.*

———◆———

Q. In what Denver museum can you watch a laser show?

A. The Museum of Natural History.

———◆———

Q. What bagpipe band from London, England, played at the Denver Municipal Auditorium in March 1985?

A. The Black Watch (from Her Majesty's Service).

———◆———

Q. What television movie starring Sam Elliot was shot in part at Buckskin Joe's near the Royal Gorge in 1990?

A. *Connagher.*

———◆———

Q. Where in Colorado did William Shatner perform excerpts of Shakespeare in 1977?

A. The Boulder Auditorium.

# HISTORY

## C H A P T E R   T H R E E

**Q.** How old was David Moffat, of Moffat Tunnel fame, when he came to Denver?

**A.** Twenty-one.

———◆———

**Q.** What was the name of the horse that pulled the railcar from Englewood to Cherrelyn Village?

**A.** Quickstep.

———◆———

**Q.** What did the engine called Dinky help haul?

**A.** Sugar beets.

———◆———

**Q.** What 521,000-acre bombing range was once planned to train British Royal Air Force personnel?

**A.** La Junta Army Air Field.

———◆———

**Q.** When is Colorado Day celebrated?

**A.** The first Monday in August.

**Q.** In 1980, where did Colorado rank nationwide in crime?

**A.** Fourth.

———◆———

**Q.** What Texas rancher blazed the first important cattle trail to Colorado?

**A.** Charlie Goodnight.

———◆———

**Q.** When did the United Mine Workers' union establish itself in Colorado?

**A.** 1899.

———◆———

**Q.** What was the real name of Soapy Smith, Colorado's biggest con artist?

**A.** Jefferson Randolph Smith.

———◆———

**Q.** In what year did Wells Fargo make its first run to Colorado?

**A.** 1865.

———◆———

**Q.** By what other name was Margaret Tobin known?

**A.** Molly Brown.

———◆———

**Q.** In 1878, who became mayor of Leadville?

**A.** Horace Austin Warner Tabor (mining tycoon).

**Q.** In what town was the last spike of the Kansas Pacific Railroad to Denver driven?

**A.** Strasburg.

———◆———

**Q.** Between what two towns does a narrow-gauge, coal-burning train still run, as it has continuously since 1882?

**A.** Durango and Silverton.

———◆———

**Q.** What Colorado resident was considered unsinkable?

**A.** Molly Brown.

———◆———

**Q.** What was the real name of the convicted cannibal Alfred Packer?

**A.** Alferd (not Alfred).

———◆———

**Q.** When was the Colorado State Hospital in Pueblo established?

**A.** 1879.

———◆———

**Q.** Colorado was the second state to pass its own landmark law regarding what?

**A.** The right for women to vote.

———◆———

**Q.** With what material was Mesa Verde built?

**A.** Adobe bricks.

**Q.** Employees of what company were responsible for burying powder supplies and creating the name Cache La Poudre?

**A.** American Fur Company.

---

**Q.** As a young man, JCPenney started what kind of business in Longmont that failed?

**A.** A meat market.

---

**Q.** What is the full name of the man for whom the international airport at Denver was named?

**A.** Ben Stapleton (former mayor of Denver).

---

**Q.** What was the cause of the Ludlow Massacre in 1914?

**A.** Mining strikes.

---

**Q.** Nancy Dick was the first woman in Colorado to fill what state office?

**A.** Lieutenant governor (1979).

---

**Q.** What Indian tribe made its last raid into Colorado in 1888?

**A.** The Ute.

---

**Q.** What is the oldest surviving hotel in Cripple Creek?

**A.** The Imperial Hotel (1896).

**Q.** Where can one see a cannon used in the 1862 battle against Confederate forces at La Glorieta Pass?

**A.** Camp George West in Golden.

———◆———

**Q.** What part of the Botanic Gardens was opened to the public in 1965?

**A.** The Conservatory.

———◆———

**Q.** To whom is the gateway of City Park in Denver dedicated?

**A.** Captain Richard Sopris.

———◆———

**Q.** What town was started in 1914 by and for African-Americans?

**A.** Dearfield.

———◆———

**Q.** Who became Colorado's first policewoman in the late 1800s?

**A.** Josephine Roche.

———◆———

**Q.** In what year was the first state prison opened in Canon City?

**A.** 1871.

———◆———

**Q.** What was Chief Ouray's wife's name?

**A.** Chipeta.

**Q.** What year was the Brown Palace hotel built in Denver?

**A.** 1892.

———◆———

**Q.** What year did Delta become a town?

**A.** 1882.

———◆———

**Q.** When were major silver lodes discovered?

**A.** 1864, near Georgetown.

———◆———

**Q.** Coloradan Evalyn Walsh McLean once owned what famous jewel?

**A.** The Hope Diamond.

———◆———

**Q.** How many times did Colorado apply for statehood before succeeding?

**A.** Three.

———◆———

**Q.** Who was the first black pioneer to come to Colorado?

**A.** Freed slave Clara Brown.

———◆———

**Q.** How many graduates were in the University of Colorado's first class of 1883?

**A.** Seven.

**Q.** What U.S. Army detachment from the Mexican War, affiliated with a religious group, spent the winter of 1846 in Pueblo?

**A.** The Mormon Battalion.

———◆———

**Q.** John Love left the governorship of Colorado to take what government position?

**A.** Secretary of Energy in Ronald Reagan's administration.

———◆———

**Q.** What did it cost to construct Denver's Brown Palace hotel?

**A.** $1,600,000.

———◆———

**Q.** In what year did Samuel Hartsel establish the town of Hartsel?

**A.** 1866.

———◆———

**Q.** When was the railroad station closed in Pitkin?

**A.** 1910.

———◆———

**Q.** What was Tin Cup renamed in 1880?

**A.** Virginia City (but it was changed back to Tin Cup two years later).

———◆———

**Q.** Ignoring Indian claims to Colorado land, miners set up what government that Congress refused to recognize?

**A.** The Jefferson Territory.

Q. Where and when was gold first discovered in Colorado?

A. Along Cherry Creek, near present-day Denver, in 1858.

---

Q. How many states were already in the Union when Colorado became a state?

A. Thirty-seven.

---

Q. When was Colorado Springs founded?

A. 1871.

---

Q. Where was the site of the Alferd Packer massacre?

A. Lake City.

---

Q. What mountains did the Indians call the Shadow Hills?

A. The Wet Mountains.

---

Q. What was the original name of the Arkansas River?

A. The Nepesta.

---

Q. What does the name of the town of Towaoc mean in Indian?

A. "All right."

**Q.** What town can claim to be the home of Colorado's oldest rodeo?

**A.** Monte Vista.

---◆---

**Q.** What town served as capital of the Colorado Territory from 1862 to 1867?

**A.** Golden.

---◆---

**Q.** Where was Molly Brown on April 14, 1912?

**A.** Aboard the *Titanic* (she survived).

---◆---

**Q.** Who was considered to be the "Pathfinder of the San Juans"?

**A.** Otto Mears.

---◆---

**Q.** What is the name of the thirty-seven-room Victorian mansion given to Pueblo by the Thatcher family?

**A.** Rosemount.

---◆---

**Q.** Who was Mount Silver Heels named after?

**A.** A dance-hall girl.

---◆---

**Q.** What Colorado military base served as President Dwight D. Eisenhower's summer White House?

**A.** Lowry Air Force Base.

Q. A shrine honoring what Catholic saint offers a panoramic view of the Denver area?

A. Mother Cabrini.

---

Q. What president acquired present-day eastern and central Colorado for the United States?

A. Thomas Jefferson (through the Louisiana Purchase, 1803).

---

Q. Who became the first police chief of Denver in 1862?

A. George E. Thornton.

---

Q. What town was named after a tombstone maker?

A. Monument.

---

Q. What famous resident of Leadville once made the statement, "Leadville has ten months of winter and two months of late fall"?

A. Doc Holliday.

---

Q. What was the slogan of prospectors as they traveled the hard trail to the Colorado gold fields?

A. "Pikes Peak or Bust."

---

Q. When were the Denver Botanic Gardens founded?

A. 1951.

**Q.** What does the Indian word *kinnikinnik* mean?

**A.** "Bearberry."

---

**Q.** In what town is the nation's longest continuously running oil well?

**A.** Florence.

---

**Q.** What road was once described by Theodore Roosevelt as the "trip that bankrupts the English language?"

**A.** Gold Camp.

---

**Q.** Who appointed William Gilpin as Colorado's first territorial governor in 1861?

**A.** President Abraham Lincoln.

---

**Q.** In 1706, what Spanish official claimed the Colorado region for Spain?

**A.** Juan de Ulibarri.

---

**Q.** The statue of what great Colorado explorer and pioneer is in Colorado Springs?

**A.** William Palmer.

---

**Q.** How many rooms does the Cave of the Winds at Maniton Springs have on exhibition?

**A.** Twenty.

**Q.** In 1896, what plank in the platform of the Republican party caused many Coloradans to withdraw and form a competing party?

**A.** A plank favoring a monetary system based on the gold standard, which would not benefit a silver-producing state.

———◆———

**Q.** Whose presidential administration declared Colorado U.S. territory?

**A.** James Buchanan's (Feb. 28, 1861).

———◆———

**Q.** How long did it take to build the Colorado State Capitol?

**A.** Twenty-two years.

———◆———

**Q.** What is the oldest organized Hispanic group in the United States?

**A.** League of United Latin American Citizens.

———◆———

**Q.** What was the original name of the Colorado State Patrol?

**A.** Colorado Courtesy Patrol.

———◆———

**Q.** The first American party to explore the Colorado region was headed by what man?

**A.** Col. Zebulon M. Pike (in 1806).

———◆———

**Q.** What do Silver Cliff and Pueblo have in common?

**A.** They both contended to become the state capital.

HISTORY

**Q.** Why is Colorado called the Centennial State?

**A.** It entered the Union in 1876, one hundred years after the signing of the Declaration of Independence.

———◆———

**Q.** How large an area does NORAD cover?

**A.** 4.5 acres.

———◆———

**Q.** What does the Spanish word *mesa verde* mean?

**A.** "Green table."

———◆———

**Q.** What was the first army post in Colorado?

**A.** Fort Garland (1858).

———◆———

**Q.** What famous scout is buried on Lookout Mountain?

**A.** William F. ("Buffalo Bill") Cody.

———◆———

**Q.** Which U.S. president appointed Colorado lawyer James Watt as secretary of the interior?

**A.** Ronald Reagan.

———◆———

**Q.** What Colorado town is Congressman Wayne Aspinall from?

**A.** Palisade.

**Q.** What man had two towns named after him, one in Colorado and the other in Wyoming?

**A.** Casper Collins.

---

**Q.** Lewis Ledyard Weld was the first to hold what governmental position in Colorado?

**A.** Secretary of state.

---

**Q.** What Colorado railroad celebrated its one hundredth anniversary in 1991?

**A.** The Pikes Peak Cog Railway.

---

**Q.** What was the original name of Central City?

**A.** Mountain City.

---

**Q.** What automotive business once occupied the present Gates Rubber Plant?

**A.** Ford Motor Company (in Denver).

---

**Q.** What judicial office is no longer recognized in Colorado?

**A.** Justice of the peace.

---

**Q.** What mulatto mountain man constructed an adobe fortress at the confluence of Fountain Creek and the Arkansas River in 1842 and named it Pueblo?

**A.** Jim Beckwourth.

**Q.** What famous dentist died in Glenwood Springs?

**A.** John Henry ("Doc") Holliday.

———◆———

**Q.** Golda Meir, former Israeli prime minister, lived in what Colorado city as a child?

**A.** Denver.

———◆———

**Q.** In what year was the first governmental treaty with the Mountain Utes of Colorado?

**A.** 1868.

———◆———

**Q.** Until the end of World War I, what foreign investors owned 68 percent of the mining companies in Colorado?

**A.** British.

———◆———

**Q.** Who was the first white man to ascend the craggy peaks northeast of Vail?

**A.** Lord Gore (an Irish peer, in 1854).

———◆———

**Q.** What military division trained at Camp Hale, twenty miles southwest of Vail, during World War II?

**A.** The Tenth Mountain Division.

———◆———

**Q.** What town's nickname is "The Silver Queen of the Rockies"?

**A.** Georgetown.

**Q.** What candidate for the U.S. vice presidency was attacked with a broken banner pole in a Colorado town?

**A.** Theodore Roosevelt.

---

**Q.** What Nazi sympathizer in Colorado aided the escape of two German POWs from Camp Hale during World War II?

**A.** Dale Maple.

---

**Q.** Kansas Senator Robert Dole was a member of what Colorado military division during World War II?

**A.** The Tenth Mountain Division.

---

**Q.** Where did Kit Carson die?

**A.** Fort Lyon.

---

**Q.** What massacre, occurring June 15, 1864, eventually caused the Indian wars of 1864–65?

**A.** The Hungate Massacre.

---

**Q.** Where is the "Gateway to the San Juan"?

**A.** Del Norte.

---

**Q.** What town in the San Luis Valley was founded by fifty Mormon families?

**A.** Manassa.

Q. To protest inflation, what did the citizens of Central City do before the visit of President Ulysses S. Grant in 1873?

A. Temporarily paved the front walk of the Teller House hotel with thirty solid silver bricks.

———◆———

Q. What was the full name of the governor of the Kansas Territory for whom Denver was named in 1858?

A. James Denver.

———◆———

Q. Who was the last territorial governor?

A. John L. Routt.

———◆———

Q. How much did Baby Doe Tabor's wedding dress cost?

A. $7,000 (in 1883).

———◆———

Q. Who was the first white man to set foot in Colorado?

A. Coronado, the Spanish conquistador.

———◆———

Q. Who was Colorado's first woman state representative?

A. Pat Schroeder.

———◆———

Q. What battle between the Confederates and the Volunteer armies of Colorado and New Mexico took place at Glorieta Pass?

A. The "Gettysburg of the West" battle.

**Q.** How many times did James Denver visit his namesake?

**A.** Two.

---◆---

**Q.** What famous head of the Colorado Fuel and Iron Company fought over miners' wages with Josephine Roche, the first woman mine owner?

**A.** John D. Rockefeller.

---◆---

**Q.** How many members does the Colorado senate have?

**A.** Thirty-five.

---◆---

**Q.** When was the Colorado state flag officially adopted?

**A.** June 5, 1911.

---◆---

**Q.** What New York City owner of Macy's bought several mines in and around Aspen?

**A.** Jerome B. Wheeler.

---◆---

**Q.** In 1897, what famous outlaw and his gang set up camp at Powder Wash Creek, about thirty miles north of Maybell?

**A.** Butch Cassidy and the Wild Bunch.

---◆---

**Q.** What does *Anasazi* mean in the Ute language?

**A.** "The ancient ones."

**Q.** What is the name of the best producing gold mine on the western slope?

**A.** Camp Bird.

---

**Q.** Who settled the first homestead in Larimer County?

**A.** Antoine Janis.

---

**Q.** Who was Colorado's first astronaut?

**A.** Scott Carpenter.

---

**Q.** What ore is mined at Eagle Mine?

**A.** Zinc.

---

**Q.** What do the Snake, Bear, and Grand rivers have in common?

**A.** All were named by the Ute Indians.

---

**Q.** What Central City miner had a railcar named after him?

**A.** George Pullman.

---

**Q.** In the 1890s, the prevalence of such characters as Bob Ford (who killed Jesse James), Frank James, Martha ("Calamity Jane") Cannary and her pal Poker Alice, and Bat Masterson gave what town its reputation as the wildest camp in the state?

**A.** Creede.

**Q.** By what name is George Leroy Parker better known?

**A.** Butch Cassidy.

———◆———

**Q.** Where is the Hotel de Paris, built in 1875 and now a museum?

**A.** Georgetown.

———◆———

**Q.** What judge tried the case of cannibal Alferd Packer?

**A.** Judge M. B. Gerry.

———◆———

**Q.** When was the first coin minted at the Denver Mint?

**A.** 1904.

———◆———

**Q.** When did the first airplane land in Denver?

**A.** 1910.

———◆———

**Q.** The University of Colorado, Boulder, started in 1877 with two teachers and how many students?

**A.** Forty-four.

———◆———

**Q.** Who was the leader of the expedition that first climbed Pikes Peak in 1820?

**A.** Stephen H. Long.

**Q.** What company did General William Ashley form in 1822?

**A.** Rocky Mountain Fur Company.

———◆———

**Q.** What major disaster hit Pueblo in 1921?

**A.** A flood.

———◆———

**Q.** What military base was established near Denver in 1937?

**A.** Lowry Field.

———◆———

**Q.** How old was David Moffat when he organized the Denver, Northwestern & Pacific Railroad?

**A.** Sixty-three.

———◆———

**Q.** In the late 1800s, what valuable find did the Atlantic Mining and Milling Company discover in the Conqueror Lode?

**A.** Quartz.

———◆———

**Q.** What special school opened its doors in Denver in 1916?

**A.** Emily Griffith Opportunity School.

———◆———

**Q.** In 1848, the U.S. government received western Colorado according to the terms of what peace treaty?

**A.** Treaty of Guadalupe Hidalgo, concluding the Mexican War.

**Q.** Silver prospectors Bill Hopkins, Philip Pratt, and Smith Steele were the first to reach what area that is now a famous mountain resort?

**A.** Aspen.

———◆———

**Q.** Who was the first mayor of Aurora?

**A.** H. M. Milliken.

———◆———

**Q.** Who commanded Fort Garland from 1866 to 1867?

**A.** Kit Carson.

———◆———

**Q.** From about 55 A.D. to about 1500 A.D., what group of Indians occupied the site of the Dolores Project?

**A.** The Anasazi.

———◆———

**Q.** What does the color white in the Colorado state flag stand for?

**A.** The snowy mountains.

———◆———

**Q.** Where was the *Ranchland News* published?

**A.** El Paso County.

———◆———

**Q.** In what year was Cuchara settled?

**A.** 1903.

**Q.** What prominent people have stayed at Salida's Poor Farm Country Inn and Breakfast?

**A.** Denver Bronco John Elway, Lieut. Governor Nancy Dick, and Sen. Tim Wirth.

———◆———

**Q.** To what tribe do the Uintahs belong?

**A.** Ute.

———◆———

**Q.** For whom was Fort Morgan named?

**A.** Col. Christopher Morgan.

———◆———

**Q.** To what group of tribes does an Arapahoe belong?

**A.** Algonquin.

———◆———

**Q.** After his death, where did Buffalo Bill lie in state?

**A.** The state capitol.

———◆———

**Q.** Who was the first state archaeologist?

**A.** Bruce Rippeteau (1976).

———◆———

**Q.** In what year was the Denver University Law School founded?

**A.** 1892.

HISTORY

**Q.** What town was burned to the ground by more than 2,000 Cheyenne, Arapahoe, and Sioux in 1865?

**A.** Julesburg.

———◆———

**Q.** What fort was started by the Salvation Army?

**A.** Fort Amity.

———◆———

**Q.** In what town did the Church of the Brethren, also known as the Dunkards, have their first Colorado settlement?

**A.** Hygiene.

———◆———

**Q.** Who was the first mayor of Montrose?

**A.** W. Cummings.

———◆———

**Q.** What Ute chieftain signed the 1873 Brunot Treaty?

**A.** Antero.

———◆———

**Q.** What man was commissioned to explore the Missouri, Platte, Arkansas, and Red rivers in 1820?

**A.** Stephen H. Long.

———◆———

**Q.** What Central City hotel held its grand opening in June 1872?

**A.** The Teller House.

Q. How long did Colorado remain the newest state in the United States?

A. Thirteen years.

———◆———

Q. What industrial company began operating in 1868?

A. The Boston-Colorado Smelter Works.

———◆———

Q. What event took place November 1, 1887, frightening the cows of Aspen so badly that they quit producing milk for several days?

A. The first steam locomotive came to town.

———◆———

Q. How many oxen were required to transport the contents of a single railroad car?

A. Sixteen.

———◆———

Q. Who was the first dean at the Denver University Law School?

A. Albert Eugene Pattison.

———◆———

Q. Who appoints the state archaeologists?

A. The governor.

———◆———

Q. What caused a statewide depression in Colorado in 1893?

A. The collapse of the U.S. silver market.

**Q.** Who founded the city of Montrose?

**A.** Joe Selig.

———◆———

**Q.** The Chisholm Trail was named for what Cherokee cattleman?

**A.** Jesse Chisholm.

———◆———

**Q.** What town was the main way station for the Pony Express?

**A.** Julesberg.

———◆———

**Q.** What astronaut from Colorado was later elected to Congress?

**A.** Jack Swigert.

———◆———

**Q.** What Colorado newspaper was printed in gold ink in 1891?

**A.** *The Gusher*, of Cripple Creek.

———◆———

**Q.** What senator from Colorado was a candidate for president in 1984 and 1988?

**A.** Gary Hart.

———◆———

**Q.** What mine did the Rothschilds own?

**A.** The Tomboy Mine.

**Q.** What were the handles of Buffalo Bill's six-shooters made of?

**A.** Ivory.

———◆———

**Q.** What was the original function of what is now the Elks building in Pueblo?

**A.** The Hotel Numa.

———◆———

**Q.** What mountainous town was once a Ute spa?

**A.** Glenwood Springs.

———◆———

**Q.** In 1974, what entire mountain town was designated a National Historic District?

**A.** Crested Butte.

———◆———

**Q.** In 1888, what town had its buildings leveled by an explosion caused by a freight car loaded with powder?

**A.** Fountain.

———◆———

**Q.** Who discovered the torpedo fish in 1858 near Bijou's Creek?

**A.** Luke Tierney.

———◆———

**Q.** What was the occupation of Mariano Medina in the 1840s?

**A.** Scout.

**Q.** What is the Colorado state motto?

**A.** *Nil Sine Numine* (Nothing Without Providence).

---

**Q.** What was the first permanent American settlement in the Colorado region, in 1833?

**A.** Bent's Fort.

---

**Q.** Felix R. Brunot was president of what government agency in 1872?

**A.** The Federal Board of Indian Commissioners.

---

**Q.** Samuel Hartsel, for whom the town of Hartsel was named, originally came from what state?

**A.** Pennsylvania.

---

**Q.** The town of Granite, situated at the mouth of Cache Creek, was the scene of what war in 1875?

**A.** The Lake County War.

---

**Q.** What U.S. president appointed Alexander Cummings as governor?

**A.** Andrew Johnson.

---

**Q.** What county was the first to have a chain store?

**A.** Fremont.

**Q.** In 1871, what railroad completed a line to Burlington?

**A.** The Kansas Pacific Railroad.

—◆—

**Q.** In what town did the local undertaker offer party rates if all killings were scheduled on Saturdays?

**A.** Altman.

—◆—

**Q.** The national energy crisis in the 1970s resulted in a dramatic expansion of what Colorado industries?

**A.** Coal and petroleum.

—◆—

**Q.** What governor served for ten years, 1963–73?

**A.** John A. Love.

—◆—

**Q.** Who was the leader of the Colorado militia that attacked a peaceful Cheyenne village in 1864, killing nearly 300 Indians at the Sand Creek Massacre?

**A.** Col. John Chivington.

—◆—

**Q.** Who was Prunes, whose grave is marked by a monument erected in 1930 near the center of the town of Fairplay?

**A.** A mining burro.

—◆—

**Q.** Guggenheim Hall, built in Denver in 1905, is the administration building for what school?

**A.** Colorado School of Mines.

Q. What was the first hotel in Auraria, which later became a part of Denver?

A. The Eldorado.

---◆---

Q. What business establishment was Richens Wootton the first to open in Colorado?

A. A saloon.

---◆---

Q. In 1859, who started the first school for the children of gold miners at Cherry Creek (now Denver)?

A. Professor O. J. Goldrick.

---◆---

Q. Where was the meeting held, late in 1867, to select Denver as the permanent seat of state government?

A. Golden.

---◆---

Q. What Indian tribe called themselves "the slashed people"?

A. The Cheyenne.

---◆---

Q. Colorado lost 297 men during what war?

A. The Korean War.

---◆---

Q. From what town was the courthouse removed and relocated in Creede?

A. Wason.

# ARTS & LITERATURE

## C H A P T E R   F O U R

**Q.** What well-known patriotic song was inspired by the view from Pikes Peak?

**A.** "America the Beautiful."

◆

**Q.** What poet wrote "Pioneers! O Pioneers!" about early Colorado settlers?

**A.** Walt Whitman.

◆

**Q.** What author of westerns wrote a story set in Colorado titled "Night on Trapper's Lake"?

**A.** Zane Grey.

◆

**Q.** What author of *Trinity* lives in Aspen?

**A.** Leon Uris.

◆

**Q.** What Pueblo artist took actual photos and then painted stirring posters depicting the "Desert Storm" conflict?

**A.** Don Wade.

Q. The Christian Mother Goose series of books was developed by what Grand Junction author?

A. Marjorie Decker.

---

Q. James Michener was once a college professor at what Colorado college?

A. The University of Northern Colorado.

---

Q. What Colorado-based author wrote *A Century of Dishonor* and *Ramona* to protest mistreatment of the Indians?

A. Helen Hunt Jackson.

---

Q. Who was the first person to photograph the cliff dwellings of Mesa Verde?

A. William Henry Jackson.

---

Q. The seventy-five stained-glass windows in Denver's basilica, Church of the Immaculate, came from what country?

A. Germany (the Bavarian Art Institute of Munich).

---

Q. What Gunnison author is the creator of *Main Street Moves*, an acrylic abstract?

A. Joe Lothamer.

---

Q. How long did the bright orange curtain designed by artist Christo hang in Rifle Gap before the wind ripped it apart?

A. Twenty-four hours.

**Q.** Who wrote *Twilight Dwellers: Ghosts, Ghouls & Goblins of Colorado*?

**A.** MaryJoy Martin.

---

**Q.** Where was built an ice palace 450 feet long by 320 feet wide?

**A.** Leadville.

---

**Q.** How many art galleries are in Grand Junction?

**A.** Six.

---

**Q.** How many playing members are in the Grand Junction Community Orchestra?

**A.** Sixty-five.

---

**Q.** What is Colorado's oldest newspaper?

**A.** The *Rocky Mountain News*, first published in Denver in 1859.

---

**Q.** Who co-founded the Denver *Post* and started a live theater in Denver?

**A.** F. G. Bonfils.

---

**Q.** What Colorado playwright featured an invisible rabbit as a leading character?

**A.** Mary Chase (in *Harvey*).

Q. What famous picture is painted on a floor in Central City?

A. "The Face on the Barroom Floor."

---

Q. For what kind of writing is Baxter Black best known?

A. Cowboy poetry.

---

Q. What naturalist wrote sixteen books on the outdoors and climbed Longs Peak more than 250 times?

A. Enos Mills.

---

Q. What annual musical event takes place in Telluride?

A. The Telluride Blue Grass Jazz Festival.

---

Q. What Coloradan wrote *The Steel Albatross*?

A. Scott Carpenter.

---

Q. What New York City newspaper editor, who is supposed to have said, "Go West, young man," sponsored a farming colony in 1870 that eventually became a town bearing his name?

A. Horace Greeley.

---

Q. What British author was so taken by Colorado that he wrote a tale about Topaz?

A. Rudyard Kipling.

**Q.** For whom did the Windsor Hotel in Denver redecorate a suite with frescoes of cupids and Venuses in its bathroom?

**A.** Oscar Wilde.

---

**Q.** What Colorado Springs author wrote the book *Redshift Rendezvous*?

**A.** John Stith.

---

**Q.** What Pueblo artist considered himself to be the "Shaman of the Prairie"?

**A.** Orlin Helgoe.

---

**Q.** What Ridgeway artist has four of his paintings on permanent display in the Wells Fargo Museum in San Francisco?

**A.** Bill Tipton.

---

**Q.** What colorful trading post that sells supplies and Indian art was established in 1900?

**A.** Garden of the Gods Trading Post.

---

**Q.** What town hosts the Thunderbird Artists, who present the Buttermilk Mountain Festival of Fine Arts and Crafts?

**A.** Aspen.

---

**Q.** Who designed the building for the National Center for Atmospheric Research?

**A.** I. M. Pei.

Q. What Denver museum hosted the Colorado showing of the Ramses exhibition of Egyptian treasures?

A. The Museum of Natural History.

◆

Q. In what town does wildlife artist Radeux live?

A. Pueblo.

◆

Q. What Steamboat Springs author wrote a series of children's books?

A. Mary Calhoun.

◆

Q. What is the name of a song about Colorado written and sung by John Denver?

A. "Rocky Mountain High."

◆

Q. What Golden author wrote *Raise the Titanic!*?

A. Clive Cussler.

◆

Q. What American humorist described a Colorado mine as "a hole in the ground, owned by a liar"?

A. Mark Twain.

◆

Q. Who wrote the words and the music for the state song, "Where the Columbines Grow"?

A. A. J. Flynn.

Q. What world-traveling journalist and radio commentator was from Victor?

A. Lowell Thomas.

———◆———

Q. In what town can one see a tree carved to look like several giraffes standing together?

A. Sterling.

———◆———

Q. What Grand Junction author wrote the book *The Lion of Redstone*?

A. Sylvia Ruland.

———◆———

Q. What Pueblo artist is known for his beautiful watercolor paintings of colorful flowers?

A. John Wilbar.

———◆———

Q. Where is the Anderson Ranch Summer Arts Center?

A. Snowmass Village.

———◆———

Q. Georgetown is the site of what extravaganza that includes ice carvings, wine tasting, and gourmet food?

A. Culinary Arts Festival.

———◆———

Q. Who built the gigantic lighting display in the shape of a cross on the side of Lindo Mountain in the foothills of Denver?

A. Francis Van Debur.

**Q.** While hunting in Colorado, amateur photographer Theodore Roosevelt took a picture of what kind of animal, which was subsequently published?

**A.** A bobcat.

———◆———

**Q.** Who became the first president of the Denver Artists Guild in 1928?

**A.** Albert Bancroft.

———◆———

**Q.** What landscape artist, who also designed the Capitol Mall in Washington, D.C., designed the Lariat Loop Road?

**A.** Frederick Law Olmsted, Jr.

———◆———

**Q.** What Pueblo sculptor is known for his bronze vessels?

**A.** Dave Dirrim.

———◆———

**Q.** Where was the song "There'll Be a Hot Time in the Old Town Tonight" written?

**A.** Silverton.

———◆———

**Q.** Who dubbed the Colorado plains and part of Kansas the "great American desert"?

**A.** Stephen H. Long.

———◆———

**Q.** In what medium did Lydia Ruyle of Greeley create her collagraph collage of "Kindred Spirits"?

**A.** Print making.

**Q.** The Colorado Indian Market, representing ninety different tribes, is held in what Colorado town each year?

**A.** Denver.

———◆———

**Q.** What is the name of the extraordinary local art show for which Hotchkiss is famous?

**A.** The Black Canyon Painters Art Show.

———◆———

**Q.** What Colorado writer wrote *Lincoln's Dreams*?

**A.** Connie Willis.

———◆———

**Q.** Who is the editor of the Colorado Authors' League?

**A.** Syble Downing.

———◆———

**Q.** Where is the Teddy Bear Picnic held each year in Colorado?

**A.** Estes Park.

———◆———

**Q.** A statue of what black American leader stands in Denver's City Park?

**A.** Martin Luther King, Jr.

———◆———

**Q.** In 1979, what photographic artist exhibited a black-and-white study of rural Coloradans?

**A.** Nancy Wood.

Q. In what year was Colorado's first public library established in Denver?

A. 1860, seventeen years before the territory became a state.

◆

Q. What large arts and crafts show is sponsored by the Canon City Fine Arts Center?

A. Art on the Arkansas.

◆

Q. What Coloradan wrote *Hyperion*?

A. Dan Simmons.

◆

Q. What Colorado museum contains the West's most complete collection of exhibits and dioramas pertaining to the Ute?

A. Ute Indian Museum (in Montrose).

◆

Q. What art show is held in Longmont?

A. Country Folk Art Show.

◆

Q. Who wrote *Khan Persuasion*?

A. Cynthia Felse.

◆

Q. What museum that commemorates the cultures of the region's various Indian tribes is in La Junta?

A. Koshare Kiva.

**Q.** What author of the historical book *Destination Denver City* lives in Sterling?

**A.** Doris Monahan.

---

**Q.** How many architects were involved in designing the Denver City and County Building?

**A.** Thirty-five.

---

**Q.** Who designed the twin statues of children astride sea lions in the fountain of the Denver Civic Center?

**A.** Robert Garrison.

---

**Q.** Who wrote *Country Editor's Boy* and *High, Wide and Lonesome* about homestead and small-town life in Colorado, 1909–18?

**A.** Hal G. Borland.

---

**Q.** What Pueblo park also has an art museum?

**A.** Mineral Palace Park.

---

**Q.** John Gaw Meem designed what Colorado Springs building?

**A.** The Colorado Springs Fine Arts Center.

---

**Q.** What Colorado author wrote the book *Dragon*?

**A.** Clive Cussler.

**Q.** What is the main focus of the May Natural History Museum?

**A.** Ichthyology.

———◆———

**Q.** What was Creede's first newspaper?

**A.** *The Candle*.

———◆———

**Q.** What senator from Arizona wrote *Delightful Journey: Down the Green & Colorado Rivers*?

**A.** Barry Goldwater.

———◆———

**Q.** What book was written in 1910 by Col. William Cody?

**A.** *An Autobiography of Buffalo Bill*.

———◆———

**Q.** What art program in Crested Butte is geared toward children ten to sixteen years old?

**A.** The Creative Arts Institute.

———◆———

**Q.** In what style was Berthoud Hall built?

**A.** Italian Renaissance.

———◆———

**Q.** In what scientific field does the Arthur Lakes Library at the Colorado School of Mines have more than 126,000 volumes of specialized reference works?

**A.** Geology.

Q. What newspaper reporter won the J. C. Penney/University of Missouri newspaper award for lifestyles reporting in 1984?

A. Don Myers of the *Rocky Mountain News.*

Q. Who wrote the poem "And There Is No Night in Creede"?

A. Cy Warman.

Q. What musem near Colorado Springs houses artifacts from the Great Pueblo Period (1100 to 1300 A.D.)?

A. Manitou Cliff Dwellings Museum.

Q. Where is there a wax display of Buffalo Bill astride his horse?

A. The Buffalo Bill Wax Museum in Manitou Springs.

Q. Who painted the main art attraction at the Imperial Hotel in Cripple Creek?

A. P. T. Zurcher.

Q. Where is the famous Van Briggle Pottery Factory?

A. Colorado Springs.

Q. What Colorado author wrote the book *Neverness*?

A. David Zindell.

Q. How many people were executed at the Old Territorial Prison in Canon City, now a museum?

A. Seventy-seven (forty-five by hanging and thirty-two by gas).

———◆———

Q. In what year was the Colorado Springs Pioneer Museum established?

A. 1937.

———◆———

Q. What memorial in Washington, D.C., was built from the white marble from Marble, Colorado?

A. The Lincoln Memorial.

———◆———

Q. The Hall of the Presidents, a wax museum, is in what Colorado town?

A. Colorado Springs.

———◆———

Q. Where is the Fred Harman Art Museum where the comic characters Red Ryder and Little Beaver come to life?

A. Pagosa Springs.

———◆———

Q. What annual event in Telluride brings composers from around the world to share ideas and new music?

A. Composer to Composer.

———◆———

Q. What poet of the Old West was mayor of Canon City in the late 1860s?

A. Joaquin Miller.

**Q.** In what town does white-marble sculptor Eric Johnston live?

**A.** Redstone.

◆

**Q.** How long does the Aspen Music Festival last?

**A.** Nine weeks.

◆

**Q.** What resident of Lake City co-authored a book with Walter Bourneman titled *A Guide to Colorado's Four-teeners*?

**A.** Lyn Lampert.

◆

**Q.** What Pueblo artist made a work of art from an ammunition box by painting it with faces and a collage?

**A.** Judith Pearce.

◆

**Q.** What Colorado writer wrote the mystery novel *A Clear Case of Murder*?

**A.** Warwick Downing.

◆

**Q.** Who created the statue of *The Bronco Buster* that stands in Denver's Civic Center?

**A.** George Ridings, Sr.

◆

**Q.** What ranch worker in Blue Mountain is also a newspaper columnist and poet?

**A.** Robert A. Peterson.

Q. What is housed in the Eben Ezer All Saints Church in Brush?

A. The Danish Pioneer Museum.

———◆———

Q. Where is Al's Country and Western Museum?

A. Flemming.

———◆———

Q. What Boulderite wrote *Roadside History of Colorado*?

A. James McTighe.

———◆———

Q. Where was the 1991 Biennial International Poster Exhibit held?

A. Fort Collins.

———◆———

Q. What newspaper photographer won the Pulitzer Prize for feature photography in 1984?

A. Anthony Suad of the *Denver Post*.

———◆———

Q. What Colorado Springs author wrote *Colorado's Colorful Characters*?

A. Gladys R. Bueler.

———◆———

Q. What is the central feature of the Wintershire Festival in Central City?

A. A Victorian fashion show.

**Q.** What writer of Western fiction lived near Durango?

**A.** Louis L'Amour.

---

**Q.** What are native Puebloans John and Dorothy Mendoze known for?

**A.** Their watercolor paintings.

---

**Q.** What well-known clothes designer has a ranch in Colorado?

**A.** Ralph Lauren.

---

**Q.** Who wrote the first book about Colorado?

**A.** Zebulon Pike.

---

**Q.** What artist-sculptor took Best of Show at the 1990 Colorado State Fair?

**A.** Dave Dirrim.

---

**Q.** What poetry contest is held in Cortez each September?

**A.** The Cowboy Poetry Contest.

---

**Q.** Who built the organ whose perforated paper rolls produce the sounds of a fifteen-piece band for the Burlington carousel?

**A.** The Wurlitzer Company.

Q. What August event in Evergreen includes a judged show of paintings, photography, jewelry, pottery, and weaving?

A. Fine Arts Fair.

---

Q. Where is Western Welcome Week, a ten-day arts, crafts, and sporting events festival hosted?

A. Littleton.

---

Q. Where is Sculpture in the Park?

A. Loveland.

---

Q. The annual Christian Artists Music Seminar is held in what city?

A. Estes Park.

---

Q. Who wrote that Julesburg was the "wickedest city in the West"?

A. Mark Twain.

---

Q. What sad story was written in 1895 by Wilbertine Wilson?

A. "Snows of Yester-Year."

---

Q. How many spires are there on the Chapel for All Faiths at the U.S. Air Force Academy?

A. Seventeen.

Q. What hand-typed book about Colorado, by the earl of Dunraven, contained sketches of wildlife and scenic views?

A. *The Great Divide.*

---

Q. What Colorado Springs author wrote the book *Do You Have an Owner's Manual for Your Brain*?

A. Marina Ray.

---

Q. In what museum is the cast, reinforced-concrete sculpture by Carolyn Braakssma titled *Leg and Arm Chair*?

A. The Denver Art Museum.

---

Q. What museum has a hands-on educational theme, including a miniature television newsroom where children can run the camera, be the anchor, or report the weather?

A. Children's Museum in Denver.

---

Q. How old was Christine Collbran when she wrote "An American Girl's Trip Through the Orient and Around the World"?

A. Sixteen.

---

Q. What Trinidad artist painted Aspen's Cuchara Pass and St. Aloysius Church?

A. Clara Dunning.

---

Q. Where is the *Spirit of the Mountains*, a woodcut by Cynthia Deswik?

A. Woodland Park.

---◆---

**Q.** Famous Colorado artist Richard Thomas lives in what town?

**A.** Florissant.

---◆---

**Q.** What Woodland Park author wrote *Spirit Song*?

**A.** Mary Summer Rain.

---◆---

**Q.** What Pueblo author wrote *Bridey Murphy*?

**A.** Morey Bernstein.

---◆---

**Q.** What is the name of the book that Carol Frances Connell and Helen Connell co-authored on the history of LaSalle?

**A.** *Around and About.*

---◆---

**Q.** In what style does Sally Goble of Greeley make hand-woven clothing?

**A.** Navaho.

---◆---

**Q.** What Greeley resident is the author of the war story "Beecher Island Battle?"

**A.** Fred Werner.

---◆---

**Q.** In what medium did Susan B. Anderson of Greeley create her clay sculpture *African Meditation Peace*?

**A.** Raku.

**Q.** Where can one find a life-size bronze statue by George Lundeen entitled *The Nike Girl* commissioned by the Nike Company?

**A.** Driscol Gallery (in Vail).

---

**Q.** What married couple from Cedaredge creates pottery with Southwestern petroglyph designs and whimsical animals?

**A.** David and Suki Strong.

---

**Q.** What Boulder sculptor created the earthenware clay sculpture *Maiolica*?

**A.** Lynn Bonde.

---

**Q.** What unique mural painted by Cedaredge artist Connie Williams adorns the side of Davis Clothing in Delta?

**A.** *Labels of Delta County.*

---

**Q.** What Eckhart author wrote a history titled *Red Hole in Time*?

**A.** Muriel Marshall.

---

**Q.** What is the name of Delta's recently completed amphitheater?

**A.** Thunder Mountain Amphitheater.

---

**Q.** What southwestern Colorado artist paints mountain scenes and titles them after quotes from the Bible?

**A.** DeLora Lloyd.

**Q.** From what art school did Ray Orosz graduate in 1958, later becoming art director for the Billy Graham Evangelistic Association?

**A.** Colorado Institute of Art in Denver.

———◆———

**Q.** Where can you find Cinderella's slipper and crown in a safe deposit box?

**A.** The Children's Art Museum in Denver.

———◆———

**Q.** Who wrote the historical drama *Thunder Mountain Pageant*?

**A.** Abbott Fay.

———◆———

**Q.** Who is the editor of the southern Colorado chapter of the National Writers' Club?

**A.** Phil Cully.

———◆———

**Q.** In what town is the Sky Ute Gallery and Museum, where tribal artists display their art work and crafts?

**A.** Ignacio.

———◆———

**Q.** What style of architecture is Denver's Wellshire Country Club?

**A.** Queen Anne.

———◆———

**Q.** What Colorado artist created the life-size bronze *Casey at the Bat*?

**A.** Mark Lundeen.

**Q.** What Colorado author wrote *Neon Twilight* and *Man of the Future?*

**A.** Edward Bryant.

---

**Q.** What ancient Japanese art is used by Terry Shepherd of Cedaredge in his creation of large sculptural vases?

**A.** Raku.

---

**Q.** What seventy-three-year-old Hotchkiss artist is well-known in southwestern Colorado for her abstracts?

**A.** Dorothy Garber.

---

**Q.** What subject matter does Margaret La Bonti use in her terra cotta wall relief sculptures?

**A.** Petroglyphs.

---

**Q.** What Delta artist is well-known for his wood creation of a whale titled *Tested at 40 Fathoms?*

**A.** Al Aspenwall.

---

**Q.** What is the English title for Bill Tipton's Lakota Sioux painting *Iyuskin?*

**A.** *Happiness.*

---

**Q.** What late artist from Trinidad painted *The Stonewall Valley*, *Cathedral Rock*, and *Storz Ranch?*

**A.** Roy Mitchell.

**Q.** What town hosts the Commonwheel Artist's Arts Fair?

**A.** Manitou Springs.

◆

**Q.** Carbondale is host to what art exhibit each June?

**A.** The Visual Art Show.

◆

**Q.** Mary Hotchkiss Farmer, a descendent of Delta's original founders, paints watercolors of what main subject?

**A.** Old buildings.

◆

**Q.** What Colorado author wrote *Chances and Changes*?

**A.** Mary Elmblad.

◆

**Q.** What Parlin artist also makes moccasins and sells them nationwide to Indians?

**A.** Jack Stevenson.

◆

**Q.** In what building did the Aspen Art Museum open in 1980?

**A.** The Old Hydro Electric Power House (built in 1890).

◆

**Q.** What is the name of the watercolor depicting three mules by well-known artist Bertie Stroup-Marah?

**A.** *Executive Conference.*

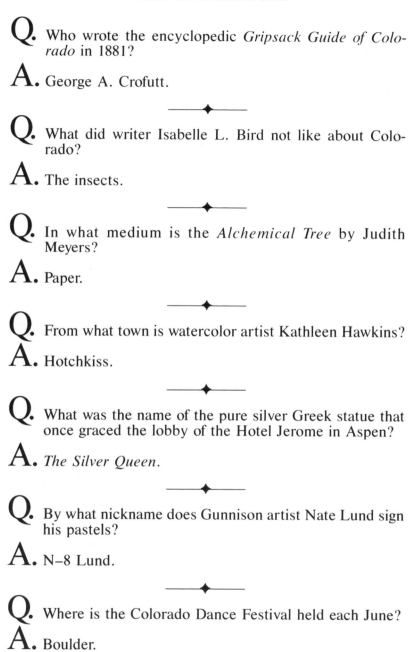

Q. Who wrote the encyclopedic *Gripsack Guide of Colorado* in 1881?

A. George A. Crofutt.

———◆———

Q. What did writer Isabelle L. Bird not like about Colorado?

A. The insects.

———◆———

Q. In what medium is the *Alchemical Tree* by Judith Meyers?

A. Paper.

———◆———

Q. From what town is watercolor artist Kathleen Hawkins?

A. Hotchkiss.

———◆———

Q. What was the name of the pure silver Greek statue that once graced the lobby of the Hotel Jerome in Aspen?

A. *The Silver Queen.*

———◆———

Q. By what nickname does Gunnison artist Nate Lund sign his pastels?

A. N–8 Lund.

———◆———

Q. Where is the Colorado Dance Festival held each June?

A. Boulder.

**Q.** Under the direction of its crusading owners, Frederick Bonfils and Harry Tammen, the *Denver Post* exposed what national scandal in the 1920s?

**A.** Teapot Dome.

———◆———

**Q.** What painting by Lee Shulin is on display at the Mitchell Museum of Trinidad?

**A.** *Colorado Clouds*.

———◆———

**Q.** What Coloradan is the author of *China Wind*?

**A.** Dan Guenther.

———◆———

**Q.** Where can one visit the Alpine Art Affair with more than one hundred artists' works on display in an outdoor exhibit?

**A.** Winter Park.

———◆———

**Q.** What is the name of the bronze sculpture by George Lundeen of a couple on a bench in Loveland's City Park?

**A.** *Departure*.

———◆———

**Q.** What was the second newspaper established in Colorado?

**A.** *The Cherry Creek Pioneer*.

———◆———

**Q.** What professional Grand Junction artist carves life-size, lifelike wooden birds?

**A.** Jim Clarke.

Q. What renowned Colorado sculptor created a life-size marble cougar entitled *Cougar Stretch*?

A. Gerald Balcian.

◆

Q. What Ute from Delta, nicknamed Nubs, painted the well-known acrylic, *Spirit Mountain*?

A. Herbert Lansing, Jr.

◆

Q. What Colorado Springs author wrote *By Death Abused*?

A. Gary Jonas.

◆

Q. What is the name of the judged art exhibit and home-made crafts fair in Fort Collins?

A. The Great Christmas Hall.

◆

Q. Artist Lydia Maurer helped design what beer label?

A. Red Lady Ale (from the Crested Butte Brewery).

◆

Q. Where is Western Welcome Week, a ten-day arts, crafts, and sporting events festival hosted?

A. Littleton.

◆

Q. What Cedaredge artist painted a watercolor of a detailed brick building with lace, gingerbread, and awnings titled *Lacemakers*?

A. Cindy Brabec-King.

**Q.** What Colorado artist created life-size, bronze sculptures of children in motion from a collection titled *Like Petals Unfolding.*

**A.** Dennis Smith.

---

**Q.** What nationally-known Coloradan created a colored pencil drawing of an Indian child titled *Walks in the Sky Horne?*

**A.** Kat Deuter.

---

**Q.** What Delta artist and onetime teacher from New York came West to become a cowboy and painted the first mural in Delta, *Delta County Ark?*

**A.** W. R. Doherty.

---

**Q.** What art exhibit in Hotchkiss celebrated its thirty-third year of continuous run June 20, 1991?

**A.** The Black Canyon Art Exhibit.

---

**Q.** What southwestern artist is known for her watercolors *Canyon Lands of Utah?*

**A.** Virginia Blackstock.

---

**Q.** What is the main feature of Sherry Cobb's pencil drawing titled *A Sudden Movement?*

**A.** A mountain lion.

---

**Q.** Who wrote the mystery *Night of Reunion?*

**A.** Michael Allegretto.

Q. What tribe of Indians is represented in painter Bill Tipton's series *She Who Has Been Chosen, He Who Chooses,* and *Happiness?*

A. Lakota Sioux.

———◆———

Q. What watercolor artist of *Stoltie Tacking Shed* is from Cedaredge?

A. Connie Williams.

———◆———

Q. What Colorado author wrote *The Fountains of Neptune?*

A. Rikki Ducornat.

———◆———

Q. What is the name of artist Glenna Goodacre's life-size bronze statue of three Indian maidens doing the Basket Dance?

A. *River Maidens.*

———◆———

Q. Gunnison sculptor Larry Runner also pursues what other profession?

A. Professor at Western State University.

———◆———

Q. What internationally-known American magazine did Arty Beal of Denver make the cover of with one of his photographs in 1988?

A. *Time.*

———◆———

Q. What Colorado author wrote the western *Ranger's Revenge?*

A. Jim Miller.

**Q.** Who wrote *Little Britches*, detailing the life on a Colorado ranch?

**A.** Ralph Moody.

———◆———

**Q.** In what month is the Colorado Art Festival held?

**A.** September.

———◆———

**Q.** What Colorado author wrote *Body of Evidence*?

**A.** David A. Van Meter.

———◆———

**Q.** The American Homebrewers Association (AHA), based in Boulder, publishes what monthly magazine whose title means the "science of fermentation"?

**A.** *Zymurgy*.

———◆———

**Q.** Where in Crested Butte is there dance, music, theater, the performing arts, and visual art?

**A.** Center for the Arts.

———◆———

**Q.** What world-famous ballet performed at the Ford Amphitheater in August 1991?

**A.** The Bolshoi.

———◆———

**Q.** What Greeley author wrote *Writing Your Life*?

**A.** Mary Borg.

# SPORTS & LEISURE

## C H A P T E R   F I V E

Q. Who started the Olympic Athletic Club in Denver?

A. Bat Masterson.

———◆———

Q. What town annually hosts the world's largest Rodeo Cowboy Association Amateur Rodeo?

A. Brush.

———◆———

Q. What is the destination town of a fifty-mile bicycle path from Denver?

A. Palmer Lake.

———◆———

Q. Who has been voted Stock Contractor of the Year for the Professional Rodeo Cowboy Association (PRCA) every year since 1987?

A. Harry Vold.

———◆———

Q. What is Colorado's oldest ski area?

A. Berthoud Pass Ski Area.

Q. What team did the University of Colorado beat in 1991 to win the national title in college football?

A. Notre Dame.

———◆———

Q. In what year did the Zephyrs hold the all-time minor league baseball attendance record?

A. 1982 (65,666 people).

———◆———

Q. What ten-day Colorado rodeo is the largest in the nation?

A. The National Western Stock Show and Rodeo.

———◆———

Q. What baseball figure, who has been fired many times, was once the Denver Bears general manager?

A. Billy Martin.

———◆———

Q. In what year did the Broncos first go to the Super Bowl?
A. 1978.

———◆———

Q. In what town did Jack Dempsey have his first fight?
A. Montrose.

———◆———

Q. What Olympic champion figure skater lives in Denver?
A. Peggy Fleming.

Q. Who won the 1990 International Golf Tournament at Castle Pines Golf Club in Castle Rock?

A. Davis Love III.

———◆———

Q. What Colorado sport uses carabiniers?

A. Rock climbing.

———◆———

Q. Who was the coach of the Denver Broncos in 1981?

A. Dan Reeves.

———◆———

Q. What heavyweight boxing champion lived in Denver at one time?

A. Sonny Liston.

———◆———

Q. How many Pro Rodeo-sanctioned events took place in Colorado in 1990?

A. Fifty-three.

———◆———

Q. What is the state's first major league baseball team?

A. The Colorado Rockies (franchised in 1991).

———◆———

Q. Steamboat Springs was the hometown of what famous skier?

A. Wallace ("Buddy") Werner.

**Q.** What is the name of the mascot for Colorado University's football team?

**A.** Ralphi.

———◆———

**Q.** What was the nickname of Dan Issel of the Denver Nuggets?

**A.** The Horse.

———◆———

**Q.** What is the term for the mark made by a skier who falls backward in the snow?

**A.** A sitzmark.

———◆———

**Q.** What kind of race is the Coors Classic?

**A.** A bicycle race.

———◆———

**Q.** At what county seat is the International Golf Tournament held?

**A.** Castle Rock.

———◆———

**Q.** What heavyweight champion boxer was born in Manassa?

**A.** Jack Dempsey.

———◆———

**Q.** What is the mascot for U.S. Air Force Academy teams?

**A.** A falcon.

**Q.** How long is the Bolder Boulder run?

**A.** Ten kilometers.

---◆---

**Q.** To what league did the Denver Gold belong?

**A.** The now defunct USFL.

---◆---

**Q.** Who was the first coach of the Denver Nuggets?

**A.** Bob Bass (1967).

---◆---

**Q.** How many times has Denver University been the NCAA hockey champion?

**A.** Five.

---◆---

**Q.** Where was the first auto dirt racetrack in Colorado?

**A.** Overland Park.

---◆---

**Q.** What Scottish sporting events take place in Golden each year?

**A.** The Highland Games.

---◆---

**Q.** What is the course of the bicycle race Ride the Rockies?

**A.** Cortez to Denver.

**Q.** In what Colorado town is a drag race through 200 feet of mud held each year?

**A.** Craig.

---◆---

**Q.** What ski resort is a part of the mine called "Little Nell"?

**A.** Aspen.

---◆---

**Q.** What mountain climbing event does Del Norte host?

**A.** The World Class Rock Climbing Competition.

---◆---

**Q.** What two consecutive years did the Mesa Mavericks of Grand Junction win the national championship in football?

**A.** 1982 and 1983.

---◆---

**Q.** What was the original nickname of Mile High Stadium?

**A.** Bear Stadium.

---◆---

**Q.** What town is host to the ten-kilometer Volksmarch?

**A.** Georgetown.

---◆---

**Q.** Where is the annual Outhouse Race held?

**A.** The Black Forest.

Q. What was the original name for the PRCA?

A. The Cowboy Turtle Association.

———◆———

Q. What Denver Bronco played in the 1985 Pro Bowl?

A. Sammy Winder.

———◆———

Q. What Aspenite came in second place in the 1990 Denver Grand Prix?

A. Danny Sullivan.

———◆———

Q. Were can one watch the Rolling Stone/U.S. Magazine Challenge ski series?

A. Aspen.

———◆———

Q. What ski area hosted the 1991 American Ski Classic?

A. Vail/Beaver Creek.

———◆———

Q. What Olympic gold medal winner for bicycling lived in Aspen?

A. Alexi Grewal.

———◆———

Q. To what sports conference does the University of Colorado belong?

A. The Big Eight.

Q. What annual car race occurs at Pikes Peak?

A. The Pikes Peak Hill Climb.

◆

Q. What was the name of Denver's professional National Hockey League team?

A. The Colorado Rockies.

◆

Q. Olympic Nordic skiing champion James Barrows was from what town?

A. Steamboat Springs.

◆

Q. Robert Bettie and Charles Ferries, on the staff of the U.S. Olympic ski team, were both from what Colorado town?

A. Boulder.

◆

Q. What 1968 Olympic champion in Greco-Roman wrestling was from Alamosa?

A. Richard Tamble.

◆

Q. What track and field Olympic champion hails from Colorado?

A. Ron Whitney.

◆

Q. Where is the Denver Tennis Open held?

A. The Denver Tennis Club.

Q. When is the Bolder Boulder race?

A. Memorial Day.

———◆———

Q. What Coloradan finished last in the 1991 Indianapolis 500?

A. Buddy Lazier.

———◆———

Q. Where is the International Hang Gliding Championship held each year?

A. Telluride.

———◆———

Q. What is Kissing Camels in Denver?

A. Golf course and country club.

———◆———

Q. What horse won the title of Bucking Horse of the Year in 1961?

A. Jesse James.

———◆———

Q. Where is the Rocky Mountain Open golf tournament held?

A. Grand Junction.

———◆———

Q. For what event did Denver's Bernard Wrightson win his Olympic medal?

A. Springboard diving.

Q. What special honor did wide receiver Steve Watson earn in his first year with the Broncos in 1981?

A. All Pro.

———◆———

Q. From what country was the 1991 Elite World Class Athletic male winner in the Bolder Boulder?

A. Kenya.

———◆———

Q. Who wears the number 7 jersey for the Broncos?

A. John Elway.

———◆———

Q. What position did Lyle Alzado play when he was with the Broncos?

A. Defensive end.

———◆———

Q. Where is the Iron Horse Bicycle Classic held?

A. Durango.

———◆———

Q. Breckenridge was host to what 1991 Broncos golf tournament?

A. The Steve Watson Golf Classic.

———◆———

Q. Where is the longest and oldest kayak race in North America held?

A. Salida.

**Q.** What was the name of the first horse inducted into the Pro Rodeo Cowboy Association, located in Colorado Springs?

**A.** Decent.

———◆———

**Q.** In 1987, who hit the longest home run (582 feet) for the Denver Bears?

**A.** Joey Meyer.

———◆———

**Q.** To what annual hill climb is Salida host?

**A.** Continental Divide Auto Hill Climb.

———◆———

**Q.** What type of race is the Copper Mountain Criterium?

**A.** Bicycling.

———◆———

**Q.** Besides a fine arts show and an amphitheater program, what sports show does the Dillon Open feature?

**A.** A sailboating regatta.

———◆———

**Q.** What PRCA event does Lamar host?

**A.** The Sand and Sage Roundup.

———◆———

**Q.** How many times have the Denver Broncos been to the Super Bowl?

**A.** Four.

Q. What position did former Broncos team member John Keyworth play?

A. Running back (1974–1980).

◆

Q. How many kilometers is the Lake San Cristobal Walk/Run?

A. Ten.

◆

Q. What international sporting event took place in Durango in May 1991?

A. Champion International Whitewater Race.

◆

Q. What Coloradan was the 1990 world champion mountain bike rider?

A. Ned Overand.

◆

Q. How many times has Bruce Ford claimed the world champion bareback riding title?

A. Five.

◆

Q. What year did the Denver Bears become the Denver Zephyrs?

A. 1985.

◆

Q. What rodeo is held annually in Grand Junction?

A. The Colorado Stampede Rodeo.

**Q.** Where is the National Off-Road Bike Association head-quartered?

**A.** Colorado Springs.

———◆———

**Q.** What was Haven Moses' jersey number?

**A.** 25.

———◆———

**Q.** Who was the female winner of the 1990 Elite World Class Athletic Bike Race?

**A.** Delillah Asiago.

———◆———

**Q.** The Denver Nuggets were one of how many teams to make the transition when the NBA and the ABA merged in the 1970s?

**A.** Four.

———◆———

**Q.** Where is the Colorado State Tennis Open held?

**A.** Gates Tennis Center in Denver.

———◆———

**Q.** In what year did the Rage in the Sage bike championships begin?

**A.** 1985.

———◆———

**Q.** What team did John Elway leave to join the Denver Broncos?

**A.** The Indiana Colts (then the Baltimore Colts).

**Q.** What Denver Bears pitcher later pitched for the Atlanta Braves?

**A.** Phil Meeker.

———◆———

**Q.** Where was the Blue Mesa Fishing Tournament held in 1991?

**A.** Gunnison.

———◆———

**Q.** What invitational golf tournament is held in Delta?

**A.** The Grand Mesa Invitational.

———◆———

**Q.** In what category did Mitch Carrier win first place in the 1990 Silverton Deer Park Hillclimb?

**A.** Expert.

———◆———

**Q.** What foot race is held in Commerce City each Fourth of July?

**A.** Four on the Fourth (a four-mile run).

———◆———

**Q.** What was the first college that former Broncos star Lyle Alzado played for?

**A.** Yankton College (South Dakota).

———◆———

**Q.** What year did Bruce Ford first qualify for the PRCA national finals?

**A.** 1979.

**Q.** How many people finished in the 1991 Bolder Boulder run?

**A.** 29,214.

---

**Q.** What Yankee shortstop and NBC sports broadcaster once played with the Denver Bears?

**A.** Tony Kubek.

---

**Q.** What was the Zephyr baseball team named after?

**A.** A train.

---

**Q.** Approximately how many tennis players play in the Denver metro area?

**A.** 86,000.

---

**Q.** What is the mucking, drilling, and gold panning contest in Idaho Springs called?

**A.** Gold Rush Days.

---

**Q.** How many wins did Colorado have in the Big Eight college basketball nonconference season for 1988–1989?

**A.** Seven.

---

**Q.** What is the official name of the De Beque's chili contest?

**A.** Woody's Chili Cook-Off.

Q. How long has the Aspen Music School held its annual music festival?

A. Since 1949.

———◆———

Q. How many times has J. D. Yates of Pueblo qualified for the National Rodeo finals?

A. Twelve.

———◆———

Q. To help the Severely Handicapped and Retarded Efforts (SHARE), a golf tournament is held in what town?

A. Westminster.

———◆———

Q. Lafayette is host to what golf tournament?

A. The Black Diamond Open.

———◆———

Q. What cross-country race at Sand Wash Basin in Craig takes place each September?

A. AMA Hare and Hound Motorcycle Race.

———◆———

Q. What All-Star outfielder for the Cubs once played with the Denver Bears?

A. Andre Dawson.

———◆———

Q. What is the official name of the BMW motorcycle race in Paonia?

A. Top of the Rockies.

**Q.** As of 1991, how many years has the Denver City Tennis Open been held?

**A.** Seventy-five.

———◆———

**Q.** Where did the Denver Broncos play their third Super Bowl?

**A.** San Diego.

———◆———

**Q.** Where is the Cherry Creek State Recreation Area?

**A.** Denver.

———◆———

**Q.** Where does the major PRCA stock contractor, Harry Vold, live?

**A.** Avondale.

———◆———

**Q.** How many people finished in the first Bolder Boulder run in 1979?

**A.** 2,700.

———◆———

**Q.** The annual Bannock Criterium brings the world's top bicycle racers to what city's downtown area?

**A.** Denver.

———◆———

**Q.** What town stages an annual bed race in honor of its last madam?

**A.** Central City.

Q. Who won the hand mucking (shoveling) event in the Hard Rockers Holidays mining contest?

A. Rick Ernst.

---◆---

Q. What town hosts Olympic-style games geared for beginners and advanced athletes fifty-five years of age or older?

A. Montrose.

---◆---

Q. For what event is J. D. Yates the youngest Coloradan to qualify?

A. PRCA National Finals (1975).

---◆---

Q. What number did John Keyworth wear for the Denver Broncos?

A. 32.

---◆---

Q. What club hosts the De Beque Grand Prix?

A. The Rocky Mountain Sports Club.

---◆---

Q. What race in the state has the most participants?

A. The Bolder Boulder.

---◆---

Q. What is the acronym—and better-known name—for the race called First in Boating on the Arkansas?

A. FIBARK.

**Q.** What remote district is considered to have the best fishing in Colorado?

**A.** Roaring Fork River.

———◆———

**Q.** Where can one ride the Coonskin Scenic Chairlift?

**A.** Telluride.

———◆———

**Q.** Where is the Tea Cup Bowl?

**A.** Vail.

———◆———

**Q.** In what year did the Broncos first play for Denver?

**A.** 1960.

———◆———

**Q.** Where was the 1991 Junior University College World Series held?

**A.** Grand Junction.

———◆———

**Q.** Who sanctions the Telluride Fat Tire Festival and Land Use Symposium?

**A.** NORBA (North American Off-Road Bike Association).

———◆———

**Q.** In what town does the annual Georgetown Half Marathon finish?

**A.** Idaho Springs.

**Q.** Where is the Rage in the Sage bike race held?

**A.** Gunnison.

———◆———

**Q.** Where did the Denver Broncos play their second Super Bowl game?

**A.** The Rose Bowl in Pasadena, California.

———◆———

**Q.** What horse was Saddle Bronc of the Year for 1962 and 1963?

**A.** Big John.

———◆———

**Q.** What is the largest cross-country race in the nation?

**A.** The Coureur de Bois (in Glenwood Springs).

———◆———

**Q.** What is the name of Vail's ice hockey club?

**A.** The Mountaineers.

———◆———

**Q.** What is the highest-scoring pro basketball game ever played?

**A.** Detroit Pistons beat the Denver Nuggets 186–183 in 1983.

———◆———

**Q.** What was the jersey number of Broncos running back Otis Armstrong?

**A.** 24.

**Q.** Where is the Old Baca House and Pioneer Museum?

**A.** Trinidad.

---

**Q.** What motor bike race does Buena Vista host each year?

**A.** Collegiate Peaks Enduro Run.

---

**Q.** From what town was world class runner Rick Trujillo?

**A.** Ouray.

---

**Q.** In what Colorado town does major stock supplier to the PRCA Mike Cervi live?

**A.** Sterling.

---

**Q.** Who wore number 7 jersey for the Broncos before John Elway had it?

**A.** Craig Morton.

---

**Q.** What Denver Bronco was chosen for the 1985 Pro Bowl?

**A.** Sammy Winder.

---

**Q.** In 1977, what team did Craig Morton leave to join the Broncos?

**A.** The New York Giants.

**Q.** In what town is Dinger's Park, where there are horsecart races held on the Fourth of July?

**A.** Silver Plume.

———◆———

**Q.** When was Hugh Bennett inducted into the Pro Rodeo Cowboy Hall of Fame?

**A.** 1979.

———◆———

**Q.** What year did John Keyworth join the Broncos?

**A.** 1974.

———◆———

**Q.** Where is the motorcycle rally Americade of the Rockies held?

**A.** Estes Park.

———◆———

**Q.** What competition of the Hard Rocker's Holidays in Silverton did Mike Foutz win?

**A.** Wheelbarrow racing.

———◆———

**Q.** Where is the York Gulch 10 kilometer Run/Walk?

**A.** Idaho Springs.

———◆———

**Q.** What kind of sports event is the High Plains Annual Open?

**A.** Horseshoe pitching contest (in Strasburg).

Q. What town hosts the Adams County Fair and Rodeo?

A. Henderson.

———◆———

Q. Where is the Tin Man Triathalon held?

A. Fort Morgan.

———◆———

Q. What pond hosts the Washington County Fishing Derby?

A. Akron Pond.

———◆———

Q. What Denver Broncos player broke the single game rushing record in 1974?

A. Otis Armstrong.

———◆———

Q. Where is the Olympic Training Center, national headquarters for the U.S. Olympic Committee and fifteen national sports-governing bodies?

A. U.S. Olympic Complex in Colorado Springs.

———◆———

Q. During what two months are the largest brown and mackinaw trout caught at Curecanti National Recreation Area?

A. May and June.

———◆———

Q. What town hosts the TDK Snowboarding World Cup?

A. Breckenridge.

Q. What Junior Olympics team qualifier for cross-country skiing is held in Carbondale?

A. Mount Sopris Classic.

Q. The Steamboat Springs Steamboat Weather Summit is for what specialized performers?

A. Television weather forecasters.

Q. What was the location of the first ski gondola in the United States?

A. Vail.

Q. At North Park, what sport is sponsored by the Jackson County Lions Club and the Walden Snow Snakes?

A. Snowmobile drag racing.

Q. Where is the Swan Song Shadow Slalom?

A. Silvercreek.

Q. To what team did Lyle Alzado go when he left the Broncos?

A. The Oakland Raiders.

Q. Competitors in the Alpine Banks Bicycle Stage Race must compete in how many separate events?

A. Three.

Q. Who was the male winner of the citizen race of the Bolder Boulder for 1991?

A. John Wessells.

———◆———

Q. What was the name of the Denver men and women's pro volleyball team?

A. The Comets.

———◆———

Q. What position did Jim Turner play for the Denver Broncos?

A. Kicker.

———◆———

Q. Where is the annual Coors/Sky Ute Stampede Rodeo?

A. Ingnacio.

———◆———

Q. What is the main sport at the Greeley Independence Stampede?

A. Rodeo.

———◆———

Q. What former Broncos player now operates a thriving McDonald's franchise in Castle Rock?

A. Billy Thompson.

———◆———

Q. In the Broncos 1977 game against San Diego, who threw two touchdown passes for a come-from-behind victory?

A. Craig Morton.

**Q.** What All-American halfback at the University of Colorado later became an associate justice of the U.S. Supreme Court?

**A.** Byron ("Whizzer") White.

———◆———

**Q.** Where can one attend the Mustang Round-up Car Rally?

**A.** Nottingham Park in Vail.

———◆———

**Q.** What Coloradan won the 1983 U.S. men's curling championship?

**A.** Don Cooper.

———◆———

**Q.** In what race do mascots of nearly fifty colleges compete in Winter Park?

**A.** The Annual University of Colorado Invitational Mascot Ski Race.

———◆———

**Q.** What is the seating capacity of Mile High Stadium?

**A.** 76,273.

———◆———

**Q.** Where does the Bud Light Half Marathon finish?

**A.** Idaho Springs.

———◆———

**Q.** Where did Bret Kimple of Denver win the 1989 Run Above the Clouds?

**A.** Woodland Park.

Q. What University of Southern Colorado student won the National Association of Inner-collegiate Athletics high jump award for two years in a row?

A. Jeff Martinez (1990 and 1991).

———◆———

Q. What was the name of Denver's onetime National Hockey League team?

A. The Denver Rockies.

———◆———

Q. What Cherry Creek High School graduate was the starting forward for the Kansas Jayhawks in the NCAA Final Four?

A. Mark Randall.

———◆———

Q. Who was the first quarterback for the Denver Broncos?

A. Frank Tripucka (1960).

———◆———

Q. What was the name of Pueblo's World Football League team?

A. The Crusaders.

———◆———

Q. In what Colorado town does Al Unser, Jr., live?

A. Colorado Springs.

———◆———

Q. What event in Estes Park sports the Caber Toss?

A. Longs Peak Scottish-Irish Festival.

Q. What unusual race is held in Crested Butte?

A. Hot air balloon.

---◆---

Q. Because it is the site of the Olympic Training Center, what town is considered the Amateur Sports Capital of the United States?

A. Colorado Springs.

---◆---

Q. What is the name of Denver's amateur soccer team?

A. The Foxes.

---◆---

Q. What 1990–91 high school valedictorian from Manitou Springs was named All-American High School Athlete?

A. Justin Armour.

---◆---

Q. As of the 1990 season, how many yards was the longest pass thrown by a Denver Bronco?

A. Ninety-seven (George Shaw to Jerry Tarr, 1962).

---◆---

Q. What was Colorado Spring's World Football League team?

A. The Spirits.

---◆---

Q. Where is the Yampa River Festival for kayak, canoe, and raft racing?

A. Steamboat Springs.

**Q.** Where are the Colorado State Parent/Child Golf Championships held?

**A.** Winter Park.

———◆———

**Q.** What race did Kurt Hoy win in 1990 for men in the 20–29 age group?

**A.** The Banana Belt Loop Race (Salida).

———◆———

**Q.** What linebacker with the Buffalos won the National Outstanding Lineback Award for the 1990–91 season?

**A.** Alfred Williams.

———◆———

**Q.** What is the name of Denver's Arena football team?

**A.** Denver Dynamite.

———◆———

**Q.** Who won first place in Denver's first Grand Prix in 1990?

**A.** Al Unser, Jr.

———◆———

**Q.** What competition did Rick Ernst and Roy Andrean win in the Hard Rocker's Holidays competition?

**A.** Machine Drilling (in Silverton).

———◆———

**Q.** What three national forests in Colorado are noted for outstanding deer and elk hunting?

**A.** Grand Mesa, Uncompahgre, and Gunnison.

Q. A main gateway for rafters and kayakers, what town is the "Whitewater Capital of Colorado"?

A. Buena Vista.

———◆———

Q. Who were the "M & M connection"?

A. Craig Morton and Haven Moses.

———◆———

Q. Cajun Ski Week is held at what site?

A. Winter Park.

———◆———

Q. Cricket, polo, and riding to hounds (despite the dearth of foxes) were pastimes at what nineteenth-century spa that was home to so many younger sons of English gentry it was known as Little London?

A. Colorado Springs.

———◆———

Q. How many municipally owned mountain areas are part of Denver's unique parks system?

A. Forty-nine (covering 24,000 acres in the foothills of the Rockies).

———◆———

Q. Who is considered the "father of bulldogging"?

A. Bill Pickett.

———◆———

Q. What is the motto of American Homebrewers Association?

A. Relax, Don't Worry, Have a Homebrew.

# SCIENCE & NATURE

## C H A P T E R   S I X

Q. Where are the headwaters of the Arkansas River?

A. Climax.

———◆———

Q. What is the only county in Colorado that has no mineral production?

A. Phillips.

———◆———

Q. What Colorado-built space unit was launched from Cape Kennedy, September 29, 1971?

A. OSO (Orbiting Solar Observatory).

———◆———

Q. What do scientists call the period in Colorado history lasting from 1 A.D. to 450 A.D.?

A. The Basket Maker Period.

———◆———

Q. Where does Colorado rank in the nation in high-tech employment?

A. Third, behind California and Arizona.

**Q.** Where is the National Asthma Center?

**A.** Denver.

———◆———

**Q.** What is the name of the think tank devoted to fostering the wise use of human and natural resources?

**A.** The Wright–Ingraham Institute (in Aurora).

———◆———

**Q.** William Richard ("Billy") Kreutzer of Sedalia was the first person to take up what profession?

**A.** U.S. forest ranger.

———◆———

**Q.** The old Denver city hall was built with stone from a quarry in what town?

**A.** Castle Rock.

———◆———

**Q.** Colorado's first sugar mill was constructed in 1899 in what town?

**A.** Grand Junction.

———◆———

**Q.** Andrew Carnegie commissioned the expedition that discovered what archaeological find in 1909?

**A.** Dinosaur bones (at the present Dinosaur National Monument).

———◆———

**Q.** How many passes in Colorado are named Ute Pass?

**A.** Five.

Q. The Thornton-based Fisher Imaging Corporation is the oldest U.S. manufacturer of what machine?

A. The X-ray.

———◆———

Q. Colorado is home to how many public and private institutions of higher education?

A. Forty-seven.

———◆———

Q. What are the Fourteeners?

A. Mountains over 14,000 feet in elevation.

———◆———

Q. What variety of grass is considered endangered in Colorado?

A. Buffalo grass.

———◆———

Q. When was the Advanced Technology Institute founded?

A. 1983.

———◆———

Q. How long is Grand Lake?

A. Twelve miles.

———◆———

Q. Among all the states, Colorado and Oregon tie for having what kind of natural resource being most endangered?

A. Rivers.

Q. Where is the largest petrified tree stump ever found?

A. Florissant (thirteen feet in diameter).

———◆———

Q. The roots of what Colorado wildflower were used by the Indians to poison their arrows?

A. The wild iris.

———◆———

Q. On what did the five Shwayder brothers stand to prove its durability?

A. A single piece of Samsonite luggage.

———◆———

Q. What Colorado soil is unusable for crops or grazing?

A. Alkali.

———◆———

Q. How many mountains in Colorado are over 14,000 feet high?

A. Fifty-two.

———◆———

Q. What town is known as the Pinto Bean Capital?

A. Dove Creek.

———◆———

Q. The town of Palisade is famous for what agricultural product?

A. Peaches.

Q. Melon and zinnia seeds are some of the major crops of what valley?

A. The Arkansas.

———◆———

Q. What South American animal is raised in parts of Colorado?

A. The llama.

———◆———

Q. Ecologically, how many life zones exist from Colorado's high plains to the high mountain peaks?

A. Six.

———◆———

Q. What group of Europeans immigrated to Colorado to become sheep ranchers?

A. The Basques.

———◆———

Q. In addition to beer, what drink did Coors bottle early in this century?

A. Milk.

———◆———

Q. What, besides oil, was called "black gold" in Colorado?

A. Beaver pelts.

———◆———

Q. What Colorado animal usually gives birth to twins?

A. The Colorado mule deer.

Q. In 1959, what huge irrigation system was completed to provide water for 720,000 acres of farmland?

A. Colorado-Big Thompson Project.

———◆———

Q. What is the meaning of the Ute word *uncompahgre*?

A. "Hot water spring."

———◆———

Q. What French scientist experimented with western Colorado ore in the early 1900s?

A. Madame Curie.

———◆———

Q. What is the pronghorn antelope popularly called in Colorado?

A. The sage goat.

———◆———

Q. What did O. P. Bauer invent in 1871 in Denver?

A. The ice cream soda.

———◆———

Q. What is the Monfort or Colorado Company best known for?

A. Beef.

———◆———

Q. What Montrose company is nationally famous for its candy?

A. Russell Stover.

Q. What Colorado produce is known as Chardonnay and Gewürztraminer?

A. Grapes.

———◆———

Q. The floors of the Colorado State Capitol are made from what type of stone?

A. Marble.

———◆———

Q. What product other than beer does Coors make?

A. Commercial ceramic parts.

———◆———

Q. Colorado leads the nation in the production of what metal that hardens steel?

A. Molybdenum.

———◆———

Q. In 1983, what winery won the award for the best 1980 Cabernet sauvignon at the San Francisco Fair and Exposition?

A. Colorado Mountain Vineyards at Palisade.

———◆———

Q. What is the present name for the substance that Colorado Indians called "the rock that burns"?

A. Oil shale.

———◆———

Q. What is the Colorado state gem?

A. The aquamarine.

Q. The first license plate on a car in the United States was seen in Denver in what year?

A. 1908.

✦

Q. *Champagne* is a popular nickname in Colorado for what kind of precipitation?

A. Powder snow.

✦

Q. What well-known cereal was first served in 1893 in Denver?

A. Shredded wheat.

✦

Q. The town of Eads is famous for raising what kind of fowl?

A. Turkeys.

✦

Q. The teeth of what Colorado animal is of a substance similar to ivory?

A. Elk.

✦

Q. What is a chukar?

A. An Old World partridge introduced into the western United States.

✦

Q. What is the nickname for the Colorado aspen tree?

A. Quakie.

Q. What are Colorado moraines?

A. Rocks left by retreating glaciers.

———◆———

Q. What animal found in Colorado is called a boar when it is a male and a sow when female?

A. The bear.

———◆———

Q. What are chimingbells and blue mustards?

A. Colorado wildflowers.

———◆———

Q. What unusual survival technique does the bird called a ptarmigan exhibit?

A. It changes colors with the seasons.

———◆———

Q. What Denver company has played a vital role in U.S. military and space programs?

A. Martin Marietta.

———◆———

Q. Red, purple, and blue describe what produce grown in Colorado?

A. Corn.

———◆———

Q. What bird did miners use to test the air inside of the mines?

A. The pigeon.

Q. What is a baby antelope called?

A. A kid.

———◆———

Q. What can give a person Rocky Mountain spotted fever?

A. A bite from a wood tick.

———◆———

Q. What native Colorado bird has a bright reddish brown tail with black stripes?

A. The canyon wren.

———◆———

Q. What is the smallest Colorado woodpecker?

A. The downy woodpecker.

———◆———

Q. What pair of insects can produce up to sixty million offspring in a single season?

A. The potato beetle.

———◆———

Q. What kind of nest does the western grebe build?

A. A floating nest (in rushes).

———◆———

Q. What is the name given to the warm wind that occasionally blows down the eastern slopes of the Rockies in winter, raising temperatures on the plains by twenty degrees in a short time?

A. Chinook.

SCIENCE & NATURE

Q. What is the popular nickname in Colorado of the junco bird?

A. Snowbird.

———◆———

Q. What do residents call the level, almost treeless areas that are surrounded by Colorado's mountains?

A. Parks.

———◆———

Q. In Colorado, what is a cayuse or a broomtail?

A. A wild horse.

———◆———

Q. What Durango-born astronaut was a crewman on the Apollo 14 space mission that made a manned landing on the moon in 1971?

A. Stuart Allen Roosa.

———◆———

Q. What animal has done more to alter the course of the Colorado River than any other?

A. The beaver.

———◆———

Q. What is the correct name for the Colorado buffalo?

A. Bison (actually, it's not really a buffalo).

———◆———

Q. What is the actual name for the "miners' cat"?

A. Ringtail.

Q. What is also known as the "Townsend's big-eared"?

A. A bat.

---

Q. What is a cony?

A. A pika, a small harelike mammal found in the mountains.

---

Q. Hares live in nests called by what name?

A. Forms.

---

Q. What fish native to Colorado is called the "cutthroat"?

A. The trout.

---

Q. What son of a Swiss immigrant, who follwed his father as head of the family's Colorado copper interests, established a foundation for the promotion of aeronautics in 1924?

A. Daniel Guggenheim.

---

Q. What four Colorado counties are the national center for production of cattle fattened in feed lots rather than on the open range?

A. Weld, Morgan, Larimer, and Boulder.

---

Q. What is the correct name for the sparrow hawk?

A. The American kestrel.

Q. What is a "Mormon cricket"?

A. A locust.

———◆———

Q. A crayfish produces up to how many offspring per year?

A. 700.

———◆———

Q. What is the correct name of the mammal colloquially called a "whistle pig" in Colorado?

A. The yellow-bellied marmot.

———◆———

Q. Whose statue represents Colorado in the U.S. Capitol's Statuary Hall?

A. Florence Sabin, who was nationally famous for her public health work.

———◆———

Q. What is unique about the Red Rocks Amphitheater near Denver?

A. It is largely a natural formation.

———◆———

Q. Who was the first president of the Denver Medical Society?

A. Dr. Richard Green Buckingham.

———◆———

Q. What invention did Nikola Tesla develop?

A. The induction motor.

**Q.** Why did the native Americans abandon their villages at the present Hovenweep National Monument in the tenth and eleventh centuries?

**A.** Extended droughts.

---

**Q.** What town is known for its melons?

**A.** Rocky Ford.

---

**Q.** What lizard is now the Colorado state fossil?

**A.** The stegosaurus.

---

**Q.** What does the Shawnee Indian word *wapiti* mean?

**A.** "Elk."

---

**Q.** What sea bird is also found in Colorado?

**A.** The white pelican.

---

**Q.** How many different species of bird have been recorded in Colorado?

**A.** 441.

---

**Q.** What color is the tip of a bobcat's tail?

**A.** Black on top and white near the skin.

Q. What is the smallest fox found in Colorado?

A. The kit fox, also known as the swift fox.

---

Q. At what altitude does the ponderosa pine cease to grow?

A. 8,000 feet.

---

Q. How many reservoirs are named Horse Creek?

A. Two.

---

Q. What Swiss immigrant built a copper smelter in Pueblo in 1888 and by 1901 was in control of the American Smelting and Refining Company, the leading company of the industry?

A. Meyer Guggenheim.

---

Q. What eerie fifty-five-square-mile national monument was formed over 15,000 years by action of the wind?

A. Great Sand Dunes (depositing sand from the San Luis Valley at the foot of the Sangre de Cristo Range of mountains).

---

Q. Where is the National Earthquake Information Center?

A. Colorado School of Mines, Golden.

---

Q. Where is the National Bureau of Standards?

A. Fort Collins.

Q. What is Colorado's state bird?

A. The lark bunting.

———◆———

Q. Where was the first tuberculosis treatment center in Colorado?

A. What is currently Lowry Air Force Base near Denver.

———◆———

Q. What research center is atop Table Mesa, south of Boulder?

A. The National Center for Atmospheric Research.

———◆———

Q. Who founded the University of Denver?

A. Rufus Clark.

———◆———

Q. How many of Colorado's top fifty exporters in 1990 were from Denver?

A. Five.

———◆———

Q. What Boulder-based company developed the "CSD Home Escort," a device that electronically monitors people sentenced to home incarceration?

A. NIMCOS.

———◆———

Q. When did Mitsubishi open its Denver-based office?

A. 1980.

Q. Approximately how many Japanese-Americans live in Colorado?

A. Seven thousand.

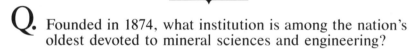

Q. What company developed a shunt for cerebrospinal fluid?

A. The Evergreen Professional and Technological Center.

Q. Ira Boyd won an engineering award for inventing what device?

A. The Humphreys spiral concentrator (an ore extractor).

Q. Founded in 1874, what institution is among the nation's oldest devoted to mineral sciences and engineering?

A. Colorado School of Mines, Golden.

Q. Melting spring snows that swell the Arkansas river to flood stage near Salida create a twenty-six-mile course for what event?

A. The FIBARK River Boat Race.

Q. What man did research on "bacteria, templates and gold islands" (using bacteria to make holes in thin metal film)?

A. Ivars Peterson (1990).

Q. Where is the highest altitude airport in the United States?

A. Leadville.

———◆———

Q. Dr. Robert Ballard is credited with what discovery?

A. The location of the *Titanic*.

———◆———

Q. What town is the home of Celestial Seasonings?

A. Boulder.

———◆———

Q. What museum, one of the largest of its kind in the country, contains the Gates Planetarium?

A. The Denver Museum of National History.

———◆———

Q. Where does the lark bunting, the state bird, build its nest?

A. On the ground.

———◆———

Q. What is the correct terminology for pulsations of water over the bed of sand, as found in the Great Sand Dunes?

A. Bores.

———◆———

Q. What was the first trade union established in America and located in Colorado Springs?

A. The International Typographical Union for Aged or Infirm Printers.

Q. John Cleveland Osgood developed what Pueblo business?

A. Colorado Fuel and Iron Co.

———◆———

Q. In what town was the Pilot Experimental Plant reopened in 1964 under the direction of the Colorado School of Mines?

A. Glenwood Springs.

———◆———

Q. What was Project Rulison?

A. An underground nuclear test.

———◆———

Q. What does the Indian word *tomichi* mean?

A. "Hot water coming from rocks."

———◆———

Q. In what year was gold first discovered in Colorado?

A. 1858.

———◆———

Q. What town is known as the Wildflower Capital of the World?

A. Crested Butte.

———◆———

Q. Where is the Southern Ute Headquarters and Tribal Cultural Center?

A. Ignacio.

**Q.** Silver Cliff's cemetery is known for what unusual occurrences?

**A.** Unexplained blue lights.

---

**Q.** What city lost almost all of its downtown district during a tornado in 1990?

**A.** Limon.

---

**Q.** Does water boil faster or slower at high altitudes?

**A.** Slower.

---

**Q.** The monkey nut tree is better known by what name?

**A.** The Russian olive.

---

**Q.** What Colorado town was named after a bird?

**A.** Eagle.

---

**Q.** What is the most common fish found in Colorado?

**A.** The rainbow trout.

---

**Q.** What was the only silver camp to remain in production during the silver panic of 1893, because its ore was of such high quality?

**A.** Creede.

**Q.** From what plant did the Indians make soap?

**A.** Yucca.

---◆---

**Q.** What Colorado town was named after a firearm?

**A.** Rifle.

---◆---

**Q.** What animal is sometimes called a bruin?

**A.** A bear.

---◆---

**Q.** What animals use the Little Bookcliff Range as sanctuary?

**A.** Wild horses.

---◆---

**Q.** Is the bite of the black widow spider worse from the male or female?

**A.** The female.

---◆---

**Q.** The theory of "nuclear winter" was first hypothesized at what scientific research center?

**A.** The National Center for Atmospheric Research (NCAR).

---◆---

**Q.** What is the name of the blue wasp with rust-colored wings?

**A.** The tarantula hawk.

Q. What is the name of the first butterfly seen in spring which has dark purplish brown wings with yellow borders?

A. The mourning cloak.

---◆---

Q. What is the common name for the illness that people suffer when they become dizzy after exertion in the high country?

A. Altitude sickness.

---◆---

Q. What refinery blew up several tanks in 1976?

A. Conoco.

---◆---

Q. What is the name of Colorado's nuclear power plant?

A. Fort St. Vrain Power Plant.

---◆---

Q. During a flood in 1965, what valuable animals were lost in Engelwood?

A. Nearly all the horses at the Centennial Race Track.

---◆---

Q. What variety of wren can live up to 12,000 feet in the mountains?

A. The rock wren.

Q. In Audubon history, which bird's singing was described as "singing as if it's teeth were clenched"?

A. The warbling vireo.

———◆———

Q. Which swallow has a squared tail?

A. The cliff swallow.

———◆———

Q. What baby-carrier factory is located in Evergreen?

A. Snugli.

———◆———

Q. How many different species of owl are found in Colorado?

A. Fourteen (as of 1964).

———◆———

Q. What is a Folsom Point?

A. A type of arrowhead.

———◆———

Q. What is the smallest variety of the shrike bird?

A. The loggerhead.

———◆———

Q. What Colorado pine has edible seeds?

A. The pinon pine.

Q. What son of a Swiss immigrant, who was in charge of the family's Pueblo copper smelter, set up free dental clinics in New York City in 1929?

A. Murry Guggenheim.

---

Q. What is the source of Boulder's water, said to be the cleanest and purest in the nation?

A. A glacier.

---

Q. What is the correct name for the "mud hen"?

A. American coot.

---

Q. What valuable animal is raised in Colorado for its fur?

A. The mink.

---

Q. Where is Colorado's Eastman Kodak plant situated?

A. Windsor.

---

Q. Where is the Colorado-based Neo-Plan Bus plant?

A. Lamar.

---

Q. Where in Douglas County are fossilized shark teeth on display?

A. Perry Park.

**Q.** What world's largest and most energetic partical accelerator did Colorado lose its bid for?

**A.** The Superconducting Super Collider.

---◆---

**Q.** According to the Latin Chamber of Commerce, how many Hispanic businesses are there in Colorado?

**A.** 700.

---◆---

**Q.** What bird is nicknamed the "cock of the plains"?

**A.** The sage grouse.

---◆---

**Q.** How many different kinds of pine, fir, and spruce trees are there in Colorado?

**A.** Ten.

---◆---

**Q.** What Colorado pioneer, fur trader, and merchant had a nuclear power plant named for him?

**A.** Ceran de Saint Vrain.

---◆---

**Q.** What town has the Radar Bomb Scoring Unit of the USAF?

**A.** La Junta.

---◆---

**Q.** What company, once in Boulder, now operates in Grand Junction producing down-filled clothing?

**A.** Frostline.

**Q.** The oldest known fossilized flower can be found in what museum?

**A.** Dinosaur Valley Museum (in Grand Junction).

———◆———

**Q.** The descendants of what fossilized insects first discovered in Colorado still exist?

**A.** Cockroaches.

———◆———

**Q.** Within Rocky Mountain National Park, how many peaks reach elevations of 12,000 feet or higher?

**A.** Seventy-six named peaks.

———◆———

**Q.** The Plains Conservation Center, which cares for deer, owls, and other wildlife, is in what Colorado town?

**A.** Aurora.

———◆———

**Q.** What is another name for a catamount?

**A.** Mountain lion.

———◆———

**Q.** Where did the world's first liver transplant take place?

**A.** University of Colorado Medical Center in Denver.

———◆———

**Q.** Who designed Denver's sewer system and was also the first head of surgery at the University of Colorado Medical Center?

**A.** William R. Whitehead.

Q. The first aneurysm operation was performed in 1949 in what Colorado town?

A. Fort Logan.

---

Q. Who successfully completed the first thyroid implant surgery in 1949?

A. Dr. Henry Swan.

---

Q. The pogo is what species of insect?

A. Ant.

---

Q. Who found the first massive mastodon remains in Colorado?

A. David P. Long.

---

Q. The first underground detonation of a nuclear device in Colorado took place at what federal research center?

A. Anvil Points.

---

Q. The first observatory with a telescope west of the Mississippi River was built on what Colorado mountain?

A. Lookout.

---

Q. What is also known as the Rocky Mountain canary?

A. The burro.

Q. What is the Colorado state animal?

A. The bighorn sheep.

---◆---

Q. What is the correct name for "fool's gold"?

A. Pyrite.

---◆---

Q. Who was the first woman to run a mine?

A. Josephine Roche (started in 1928).

---◆---

Q. What United States facility in Denver is one of three such facilities across the nation?

A. The Denver Mint.

---◆---

Q. How high above sea level are the valleys within Rocky Mountain National Park?

A. About eight thousand feet.

---◆---

Q. How many different species of bat are there in Colorado?

A. Eighteen.

---◆---

Q. What foundation established in 1925 annually grants fellowships to scholars, scientists, and artists so they can continue their work?

A. John Simon Guggenheim Memorial Foundation (by Senator and Mrs. Simon Guggenheim).

Q. What is the least common owl in Colorado?

A. The barred owl (last seen in 1965).

---◆---

Q. Automobiles accounted for how many deaths in Colorado in 1990?

A. 544.

---◆---

Q. How many different species of hummingbird are there in Colorado?

A. Seven.

---◆---

Q. How many different species of large wildcat are there in Colorado?

A. Three (the lynx, the mountain lion, and bobcat).

---◆---

Q. What Colorado Company built the Mariner Space Probe?

A. Martin Marietta.

---◆---

Q. For what commercially grown flower seed is Otero County known?

A. Zinnia.

---◆---

Q. Where was the first junior college established in Colorado?

A. Trinidad.

**Q.** Where is the Coor's brewery?

**A.** Golden.

———◆———

**Q.** What is a sego lily?

**A.** A wildflower.

———◆———

**Q.** What law enforcement academy is in Golden?

**A.** The Colorado Law Enforcement Training Academy (CLETA).

———◆———

**Q.** How many mineral springs, both medicinal and recreational, are in the immediate vicinity of Steamboat Springs?

**A.** 157.

———◆———

**Q.** How many different species of fox are there in Colorado?

**A.** Four (kit, grey, red, and swift).

———◆———

**Q.** What is another name for the short-tailed weasel?

**A.** Ermine.

———◆———

**Q.** Who proposed to the Colorado Forestry Association that the Botanical Gardens be established?

**A.** Kathryn Kalmbach (in 1941).

Q. What is the primary function of the U.S. Geological Survey laboratory near Creede?

A. Studying the formation of ore deposits.

———◆———

Q. The silver of the mines in Mineral County were formed how long ago?

A. 25 million years.

———◆———

Q. Of what rare mineral are the wainscoting and pilasters of the state capitol made?

A. Colorado onyx.

———◆———

Q. What kind of fossils are found in silver deposits?

A. Plant fossils only (the medium is too alkaline for animal fossils).

———◆———

Q. What is the Colorado state flower?

A. Rocky Mountain columbine.

———◆———

Q. What is the average humidity for Colorado, measured at noon?

A. 38 percent.

———◆———

Q. After gold and silver, what is the next most produced ore in Colorado?

A. Zinc.

Q. While the Eastern Slope covers almost two-thirds of Colorado's land area, it receives what proportion of surface water (the runoff of snow and rain)?

A. Less than one-third.

---◆---

Q. In what year was the first commercial radio license issued in Colorado?

A. 1922.

---◆---

Q. What major technological advancement came to the Denver area in 1883?

A. Electric lights.

---◆---

Q. In 1907, what commodity did Colorado lead in production for the whole United States?

A. Beet sugar.

---◆---

Q. The quaking aspen belongs to what family of tree?

A. Poplar.

---◆---

Q. What reptile is highly indigenous to Colorado?

A. The prairie rattlesnake.

---◆---

Q. What Colorado city is considered the hub for the development of the West's energy resources?

A. Denver.

Q. When was the Colorado State Hospital, in Pueblo, established?

A. 1879.

---◆---

Q. What is the number one cause of death for cats in Colorado?

A. Accidents.

---◆---

Q. What insect did prospectors once study to aid in the location of Colorado gems?

A. Ants (by examining the anthill material).

---◆---

Q. In what year was Colorado's Department of Wildlife established?

A. 1919.

---◆---

Q. What Colorado ore was used in the first atomic bomb?

A. Uranium.

---◆---

Q. What domesticated animal outnumbers all others in Colorado?

A. Dogs.

---◆---

Q. In what year was the Colorado Department of Health established?

A. 1876.